W9-CPC-725

The POWER of Joy in GIVING to ANIMALS

LINDA R. HARPER, PH.D.

Foreword and Contributions by
FAITH MALONEY

ISBN-13 (trade paperback): 978-0-9913340-3-2
ISBN-13 (eBook): 978-0-9913340-2-5

Contributions by Faith Maloney
Edited by Elizabeth Doyle, Virginia Kelly, and Bri Bruce
Cover design by Bri Bruce
Illustration courtesy Shutterstock, Inc.

Published by CAP Publishing

Dedicated to those dedicated to helping animals.

For dedicated Nina,
With appreciation
for all you do to
keep things going
for our furry
friends.
Linda R Harper

ACKNOWLEDGEMENTS

From start to finish, the power of joy has been my guide in writing this book. It was written with no time constraints, deadlines, self-expectations, or any kind of pressure that would detract from the experience of fully embracing every moment of this project. It seemed as if whatever the book needed to grow and develop, it presented itself just at the right time.

Faith Maloney and I always enjoy brainstorming—it comes naturally to us and we were always amazed at how easily the ideas flowed and the answers appeared during this project. I am grateful for her unwavering support and help throughout this book's entire journey and especially for her foreword and contributions to the book.

Special thanks to Elizabeth Doyle who brought joy and laughter to the editing process as well as invaluable ideas and suggestions—more than any writer could ever even imagine. I want to also extend my gratitude to another editor and animal advocate, Virginia Kelly, who also generously shared her talents in polishing the book. A very special thank you to my extremely competent and creative consultant and editor, Bri Bruce. The unique gifts that she contributed not only provided the finishing touches and steps needed to get this book out there, but working with her brought the power of joy to the entire process.

Last, but certainly not least, thank you to my entire family who has always been supportive of my writing.

PRAISE FOR
The Power of Joy in Giving to Animals

What a wonderful and timely message! Everyone who shares their lives with animal companions will benefit from the new insights and personal stories in this soul-searching book. By sharing experiences that will feel familiar to you, Faith and Linda open our minds and hearts to the power of recognizing our place in the journey of an animal's life—and their place in ours. It is, as the book says, "profoundly liberating" to allow our "best selves" to be present in our work and families. This is an outstanding follow-up to Give to Your Heart's Content . . . Without Giving Yourself Away.

- Tiffani Hill, CVA, Volunteer Program Director, Animal Shelter Assistance Program

Animal advocates don't typically realize that taking care of their needs first is vital to providing excellent care to the animals. The Power of Joy in Giving to Animals *combines wisdom and humor as it leads the reader through the efforts and rewards of balancing personal, professional, and animal advocate priorities.*

- Robin Sweeney, Executive Director, As Good as Gold: Golden Retriever Rescue of Illinois

I loved it! Very well written and organized. The information will definitely be helpful to people and the animals they love.

- Cathie Myers, Sr. National Events Specialist, Best Friends Animal Society

The Power of Joy in Giving to Animals *is truly a must read for every animal rescuer. The information, stories, and support Linda and Faith share refresh and provide balancing strategies for this journey of the soul we in animal rescuers choose to live. We are all on this journey due to our deep love for animals. This love should unify, not isolate us; motivate, not incapacitate us.* The Power of Joy *can help guide you back on the path to save or continue to save more animals rather than burning out with the inevitable sadness or grief. If you think you're too busy or overwhelmed and can't take a moment away from working with the animals to read this, then this book is definitely for you!*

- Jamie Lyn Rubin, New York City Programs Manager, Best Friends Animal Society

The Power of Joy in Giving to Animals *is much more than just any self-help type book. Wonderful information and message. I am going to do my best to apply it to my everyday life and keep my JOY. Great book—good for everyone!*

- Kelly Evans, President of Catoosa Citizens for Animal Care, Ringgold, Georgia

Stepping back from the abyss of animal welfare burnout requires first understanding what has happened to you and why. The Power of Joy in Giving to Animals *guides you in this crucial first step, and then suggests general and specific coping mechanisms so you can help yourself and continue to help the animals.* The Power of Joy in Giving to Animals *is a must-read if you are involved in animal welfare at any level.*

- Robert Blumberg, Co-Founder, Tsunami Animal-People Alliance and Middle East Network for Animal Welfare

Attending one of Linda and Faith's Giving Heart retreats literally changed my life and ultimately the lifesaving results at our shelter. So I could hardly wait to add their new book to my stress- and burnout-buster toolkit. This uplifting yet practical book is one to keep (and share) for its unique and universal insights, honest and easy-to-relate-to personal stories, and myriad proven strategies that can help combat the debilitating "compassion fatigue" that every one of us in the animal welfare world face at one point or another. Thank you, Linda and Faith!

- Elaine Johnson-Craig, Board Member/Donor Relations, Roice-Hurst Humane Society, Grand Junction, Colorado

Congratulations on a readable, engaging masterpiece! What I love about the book is that anyone, no matter where they are in their animal-loving journey, will be able to find themselves somewhere in here—AND then find easy-to-understand, practical, doable strategies to help themselves and, thus, be better able to help the animals. All of the personal stories and quotes, both from Linda and Faith as well as all the others they've referenced, allow the reader to find stories and experiences that match their own, to see they are not alone and others have been there, too. I loved it. Thank you!

- Ellen Gilmore, Employee Training and Development, Best Friends Animal Society

Everyone in animal welfare should read this book to keep them fit and ready for action. Faith and Linda are dedicated to helping those that help animals and that devotion transfers to these pages.

- Rick DuCharme, Founder/CEO, First Coast No More Homeless Pets, Inc

Table of Contents

The Power of Joy in Giving to Animals

FOREWORD

I met Linda many years ago when she came to Best Friends Animal Sanctuary to attend the workshops we offer for people interested in starting an animal sanctuary. I learned that Linda was a clinical psychologist, working to help people with their problems, as well as someone, along with her husband, Mario, who wanted to help animals. As often happens in life, we lost contact. I was working here in Utah, at Best Friends, and Linda was continuing her therapy practice in Illinois. We re-connected at the No More Homeless Pets conference in Chicago back in 2001 where Linda showed me her book *Give to Your Heart's Content...without Giving Yourself Away*. "This is it!" I exclaimed. I knew that this was the knowledge I wanted to bring to the animal welfare movement. I had done a brief presentation on burnout at the Chicago conference, but without a background in psychology I was flailing around in the dark. I knew what it felt like to be burned out, but how to come out of it was not as clear to me. Linda offered me that piece.

We worked on a presentation together for the next conference later that year—and that is really where this book had its start. We laugh about it now, but at that time I was the burnout specimen and Linda the caring counselor who was able to show me, and others like me, the light at the end of the tunnel. It worked beautifully.

Then Linda created a nonprofit organization, Blessed Bonds, in 2004. It was her way to help people and their animals stay together in crisis. Not quite overnight, but sooner than Linda would have liked, we stood before our audiences at the No More Homeless Pets conferences as two burnout specimens, one of whom was also a very wise psychologist. There is nothing like knowing a problem from the inside out to get a handle on it.

This book is a product of over a decade of presenting at conferences, in both the US and overseas, workshops at shelters around the country and other countries, retreats at Best Friends in Utah, and lots of individual counseling on both our parts. We have met thousands of people who love animals but want to find ways to help them without sacrificing their lives and sanity along the way. We know you, our reader, very well. You are like Linda and me. You are like the people who fill the room at conferences, who come to the retreats, who live and work with animals all over the globe. We are all the same. And we all matter.

Our wish is that this book will guide you through the discovery of your own way to live a fulfilled life as both an animal lover and as a happy person who continues to help animals.

Faith Maloney
November 2013

INTRODUCTION

Since you were drawn to this book, we know that you have already experienced the unique loving relationships and sense of purpose that a life shared with animals can offer. Joy abounds when giving to animals! While joy means different things to different people, Faith and I describe it as a deep sense of contentment that is always present when one's innermost desires are honored. Since it is in your heart to give to the animals, and you are doing just that, then we know that there is an underlying joyfulness in your everyday life—even in the most challenging times.

Do you enjoy an inner peace and contentment each day, or do you, like so many others who give to animals, find yourself sad, depleted, and overwhelmed? In trying to do all that you want to do, you may be taking on more than you can comfortably handle. In other words, your heart is larger than your hands. This imbalance created by not taking care of yourself when giving to animals keeps you from experiencing the vast joy that each day offers.

The Power of Joy in Giving to Animals is designed to help you find all of the joy that is already present in your everyday life. Balancing the unique needs and desires of your heart will not only make your life more enjoyable, but it will allow you to be at *your* best when helping animals. The ancient wisdom of the *Tao Te Ching* so eloquently reminds us in verse sixty-seven that if you are "compassionate toward yourself, you reconcile all beings in the world." Restoring balance from within allows us to uncover the power inside each and every one of us to help animals. While joy is a natural result of giving from one's innermost desires, its power extends far beyond the personal experience of peace of mind and contentment. Joy is a compelling, self-perpetuating, and contagious energy. It is an irresistible force that influences, attracts, and unites people working together toward a shared vision.

The Power of Joy in Giving to Animals describes the unique characteristics of animal advocates, people with a deep desire to give to animals, and the challenges that they face on this heartfelt journey. It offers balancing strategies that replenish the animal advocate's heart and that help keep it open to receive all the gifts of love, peace of mind, and immeasurable joy. Lastly, this book offers a glimpse of the incredible power of that joy and the possibilities that emerge when all who give to animals are at their best, working together to create a better world for all living beings.

This manuscript has been writing itself for many years through the conversations Faith and I have had with people from around the world—all with the shared desire to make a difference in the lives of animals. Interspersed throughout the book are quotations from animal advocates we have met along the way at our talks, sessions, workshops, and retreats. Italicized print will alert you to the thoughts, feelings, and stories they have shared with us about their experiences in helping animals. Their words may sound familiar to you. Don't be surprised if you feel that they are your own expressions. While each journey is unique, it is reassuring to remember that we are all traveling this path together. In addition to the foreword and her own story, Faith's commentaries can also be found in the sections entitled "Take it from Faith." In these writings, she takes a look at the strategies addressed in each chapter and integrates her own experiences with what she has learned through her observations and interviews with others. We'll begin by sharing our personal stories, starting with Faith, that describe the road to depletion and back that each of us took while following our desires to give to animals.

FAITH'S STORY

I was terrified of dogs as a young child and would walk blocks to avoid any dog I saw on my way home from school. My mother, a great animal lover, thought this was very silly and we got our first dog, Prudence, a terrier mix, when I was around eleven years old. It worked. I stopped being afraid of dogs, but it took a number of years for me to find my passion for them. My first love as a grown up was aptly named Prince Charming. He was a six-pound, three-year-old all-black Chihuahua. He seemed an unlikely hero, but he was just that for me. He came from the Arizona Humane Society and he selected me to be his new person. Prince taught me about dogs and through him I started to see the problems that all homeless dogs face.

In 1984, a mother of three almost grown children, I was one of the group of like-minded people who started Best Friends Animal Society in Kanab, Utah. I had some limited exposure to animal welfare from working with a small rescue group in Pennsylvania in the 1970s, but that was mostly a lesson in how not to do things. We had too many animals, not enough people, and not enough money. Looking back, although it was painful at the time, I'm glad I had that early experience. I took on this new project feeling like I knew what was needed in order to do this work properly: the right number of animals, people, and money.

But knowing something and doing it are two different things. It wasn't long before those of us at Best Friends entered a phase where we had too many animals, too few people, and dwindling funds. However, my challenge in those early days was not any of those issues; it was dealing with the people who didn't want their dogs, abandoning them or doing cruel things to them.

Animals are easy for me, even the difficult ones. Taking care of them was no burden. There is so much joy in seeing how animals live their lives. They are the best teachers of how to live each moment to its fullest, with no looking back at the mistakes of the past or speculating about the future. During this time, the animals kept me grounded. The gap between how I saw animals and how so many others saw them was vast, but I also met people who thought like me and who took wonderful care of their animals. And best of all, I was meeting hundreds of animals who, in spite of what they had put up with from us humans, were forever loving and forgiving.

But I reached a point when I needed to step back. My friends and co-workers could see I was wound up and angry all the time because of my disillusioning interactions with so many people. Stepping back and gaining perspective helped a lot. I began to see that our whole society is distorted when it comes to how to care about and even think about animals. Our town of Kanab and the surrounding area in Southern Utah had a long farming and ranching tradition. Animals were seen as a product for the table or as an assistant on the ranch: a working cattle dog or a mouser to keep the rodents out of the barns. To me, animals are more than that. I was not against a dog or a cat or a horse having a job, but seeing the animal as a born servant can lead to abuse and neglect. Still I could understand that a good working dog could be a valuable asset on the ranch; a good mouser was worth her weight in gold.

I saw the same thinking when I lived in rural Pennsylvania so I knew it was not just a local issue. By seeing the larger picture, I was able to see the individuals with whom I was so angry as reflections of their culture. Knowing that we are all shaped by whatever belief systems we are raised in helped me find my way back. In seeing the larger picture, I was able to understand and even forgive a lot of what I saw in how people took care of animals. And if I was going to change it, being angry and hateful all the time was not going to make that happen.

LINDA'S STORY

Looking back on my childhood, my passion for animals goes back as far as I can remember. At age three, my favorite possession was an old wooden picnic basket filled with a variety of small plastic animal figures, including cows, horses, ducks, dogs, and cats. My sister and I "rescued" abandoned stuffed animals at the local thrift shop. By age seven, fascinated by farms, my ambition was to become a "milkmaid." When those dreams were shattered by the invention of milking machines I began to design kennels for the future animal shelter I envisioned. I was twelve years old when I had a career-changing discussion with my dad about my desire to help animals. His advice was to consider "helping people first, then the animals." Although at the time I did not realize the significance of his statement or the depth of his fortuitous wisdom, I remember deciding that day to become a psychologist and "help people first." Thirteen years later I became Dr. Linda. My husband, Mario, (also a clinical psychologist) and I have had a private practice in the Chicago area for over thirty years.

Still, throughout my life, I have been involved in animal welfare, from finding homes for strays on the street to volunteering in a variety of ways at local animal shelters. I attended workshops and conferences to learn more about animal welfare. I enthusiastically became part of the growing movement to save and value the lives of animals by becoming an advocate for them. In 2000, I attended How to Start Your Own Sanctuary at Best Friends Animal Society (where Faith works). Two years later I began working with Faith to help fellow animal lovers cope with their emotions, including, burnout, anger, grief and loss, and dealing with difficult people.

In early 2004, I founded Blessed Bonds, a nonprofit organization dedicated to preserving the human-animal companion bond and promoting its value. The organization's mission is to keep people and pets together by providing temporary foster care with the intent of returning the pets back to their families. As the director of Blessed Bonds for seven years, I was immersed in its operation. I answered phone calls of desperate owners, recruited and screened pet foster and adoptive homes and volunteers, planned fundraising events and yearly budgets, picked up dogs and cats at midnight, attempted to keep paperwork straight, and performed countless other activities required to run a charitable all-volunteer organization.

I wasn't prepared, however, for managing the stress I felt or the emotional "ups and downs" I experienced every day. Although just a few years earlier I had written a self-help book about the importance of keeping the giving heart nurtured, I did not take care of myself or set limits. Joy and peace of mind were blocked by my anxiety, guilt, and the nagging thought that I was still not doing enough to help. I became overwhelmed, exhausted, and completely depleted before realizing change was essential if I was going to continue to help animals. So I found a well-established animal shelter that embraced the mission of my organization and absorbed the program. As a result, thankfully, both Blessed Bonds and I were able to survive, thrive, and continue my mission to help animals.

My journey of giving to animals has changed direction, and I now realize that my dad's simple three little words to me forty-four years ago, "help people first," may have actually reflected his exceptional intuition about my natural gifts and purpose. It was only when I hit bottom myself that I realized I also needed to include *myself* in that group of people who needed help. This simple truth then became evident: When people are helped, so are the animals. A depleted giving heart has costs greater than just one's physical and emotional wellbeing; it means one less person becomes available on this Earth to help animals. To preserve each and every person's ability to share his or her unique gifts, a replenished body, mind, and soul are essential. It starts with the individual. We must begin within and help ourselves first. Fully recovered from my depletion, I am now wholeheartedly able to embrace my journey's new direction with a renewed spirit. Drawing on my personal experience along with my professional expertise, I realize that the best way for me to help the animals is to help save the people who save the animals; each one of us matters.

FAITH AND LINDA'S JOURNEYS INTERSECT

So when Faith and I began our workshops, Faith was the burnout specimen and I was the expert psychologist. Faith found her way back, and then I became the model for a depleted giving heart. Now, with both of us coming from a place of replenishment, we are stronger than ever in our conviction to help others find balance within themselves, so that they, too, can uncover the unfailing joy that is always present in their purpose-driven lives of helping animals. When advocates are at their best more animals are ultimately helped and joy flows naturally and abundantly.

Begin within. Turn the page and take the first step toward the newly uncovered joy that awaits you, the animals, and all living beings.

CHAPTER I: THE ANIMAL ADVOCATE

WHO YOU ARE

Let's begin your new journey with a better understanding and appreciation of what it means to be a person who loves animals and is committed to improving their lives. Advocates can be defined as people who feel loving concern as well as some responsibility for the wellbeing of animals; they can be known by many different titles, including animal welfare worker, activist, rescuer, caregiver, rehabilitator, veterinarian, volunteer, consultant, pet walker, pet owner, or companion. Any number of animals may be included in the advocate's circle of concern, whether it's just a few pets, a farm full of animals, or those in need of rescue around the globe.

The activities of individuals who are committed to improving lives may range from working behind the scenes with minimal direct animal contact to direct involvement with many animals every day. While there are many ways to help, what advocates have in common is an underlying concern for animal wellbeing and the desire to give them the chance to live their best lives. The degree of involvement may also vary from your neighbor with one family pet who also feeds the birds and signs a petition to save the deer, to the volunteer with a house full of pets who works late hours at the local animal shelter. What defines you, the advocate, is a loving concern and sense of responsibility toward the animals you are committed to helping. It is this drive that sends you on this unique journey with other advocates. Your soul, your deepest self, is easily touched by any involvement you might have with animals—whether you hear stories, see pictures, or experience them firsthand. Since you connect with animals from this innermost place, your soul, your natural inclination is to become involved with those that cross your path. You have a natural desire to give to the animals and a unique ability to receive the gifts that they offer in return.

Throughout our lives, Faith and I have met thousands of people around the world who devote themselves to improving the lives of all kinds of animals. From the Midwest and Southwest, where we each reside, to across the seas in the Middle East, we find that there are three common traits found in the animal advocate: idealism, realism, and sensitivity. Using the first letter from each trait creates an acronym, the IRS. Although the ways in which individuals and organizations around the world give to animals span a great range of activities, the IRS is universally present and sheds light on the nature of every advocate's path. Understanding your IRS is the first step to becoming your *best self* on this unique, purpose-driven journey.

THE ANIMAL ADVOCATE'S IRS

If you live in the United States, the thought of an IRS (Internal Revenue Service) agent knocking at your door is likely to elicit a rapid heartbeat. My anxiety level has certainly been raised at the first glance of a letter from the IRS awaiting me in my mailbox. Obviously, that's not the IRS we're talking about, but there is a connection. By using the initials of the Internal Revenue Service, I am drawing your attention to the fact that the initials are fittingly the same as the three characteristics that make up the animal advocate: idealism, realism, and sensitivity. While this particular abbreviation is meant to serve as a memory tool for you, you may also find that your emotional response to the governmental agency is comparable to feelings that your own IRS can evoke. Understanding how your IRS functions will allow you to identify and remove the obstructing thoughts that may be blocking all the joy that this journey holds:

The Animal Advocate's IRS

Idealism: A compelling force made up of driving beliefs

Realism: The "hands on" experience and real life knowledge

Sensitivity: Intense love and compassion for animals and the ability to bond with them

Each trait carries with it components that are both positive and uplifting to the soul, as well as those that are more challenging and sometimes painful.

IDEALISM

Idealism is the compelling force that drives the animal advocate forward. The motivating power of the greater vision is evident in the following statement from an animal rescue worker: "I think No More Homeless Pets is a realistic goal and that progress is visible. That is what keeps me going." This internal force is often described as a calling that cannot be ignored. It is a passion that has led some people to quit their jobs, move thousands of miles away, and leave affluent lifestyles behind in response to a restless urge to help animals. Others play the lottery in hopes of striking it rich so they can fulfill their perceived purpose of starting an animal sanctuary. Rather than focusing on preparation for a relaxing retirement or world travels, the idealistic advocate dreams of starting and managing an organization to help animals. Year after year, this strong desire is evident at Best Friends' weeklong workshop How to Start and Run an Animal Sanctuary. It continues to fill up months in advance with likeminded participants who believe that fulfillment of their life's purpose includes starting their own animal sanctuary or rescue organization.

Another animal advocate acknowledges the more painful side of this compelling drive within when he describes his challenge: "While we are making improvements, there's suffering going on all over the planet that we may not end in hundreds of years."

Let's look at some of the underlying beliefs of an animal advocate's idealism that fuel both passion as well as disillusionment:

1. Every animal deserves an equal chance.

I dream of a kinder world for ALL living beings.

The nature of idealism keeps advocates from settling for anything less than wanting the best for every animal. When the soul is evoked there is no settling on a percentage of animals helped—every life holds immeasurable value. That belief lies in the deepest essence of who we animal advocates are. There is no changing our minds. We want every animal to have the chance to be all that each one can be in the world. One animal advocate describes this calling as "an ache that no matter how long I live, I will never be able to do for them all that they so fundamentally deserve." Another states, "Undoubtedly, the most painful [thing] is seeing the healthy animals in shelters. . . . It never fails to bring tears to my eyes . . . but provides a constant reminder of why I do what I do."

2. Everyone should share in our quest for the animals.

> *I just wish we could get more people to feel more compassion for the other lives we share this Earth with.*

In our zealous desires, we want everyone to "jump on the bandwagon," and they would in an ideal world. We believe that other people will feel just as strongly as we do as soon as we are able to convince them of what is right. Frustration occurs when idealism leads us to assume that others working for the same cause also share the same beliefs and level of commitment. One advocate states, "We need to respect each other more and get on the same page together to achieve greater results." We expect so much from the others with whom we share a passion and are often quick to dissociate ourselves from them when we feel let down. This kind of disillusionment is expressed in the commonly heard remark, "I love the animals. It's the people I can't stand." Unrealistic expectations about others often contribute to divisive conflicts between and within the animal welfare groups.

3. Truth and justice will prevail.

> *My objective is raising awareness about animals and the interconnectedness of all life in the hopes of shifting the existing paradigm.*

With idealism often comes the belief that what is right and fair will win out in the end. That belief can strengthen our perseverance and patience. Frustration occurs when the animal advocate assumes that such dedication will always result in the triumph of good. Although it seems like it "should" work this way, it is disillusioning to the idealist to find out it often does not. Anyone who has put their heart and soul into an animal cruelty case that does not go anywhere or a pet adoption that does not work out, knows the devastating disappointment when what's right doesn't win out at the end.

4. We can change the world.

> *Faith is important and we might not see the end of the road in our lifetime, but if we keep doing the work, it will come—someday.*

Making a lasting difference in the world is not too big of an expectation to the idealist. Since changing the lives of animals is on the top of your list, the idealist part of you is compelled to change the way people behave toward animals. While wanting to bring your vision to the world is certainly commendable, the expectation that others will follow our lead can lead the idealist to discontent and frustration. One such animal advocate identified her stress as stemming from "not being able to make people understand that they have a responsibility to take care of the animals in need around them—not just rely on the people who are in rescue!"

REALISM

The influence of realism on the animal advocate's desires happens primarily in two ways: through their hands-on experience, and through the knowledge that they acquire along the way. Like idealism, realism has its positive and exhilarating moments as well as painful and challenging ones. Let's look at some of the components that contribute to the animal advocate's experience of realism that fuel both the passion to help animals and the disillusionment that occurs.

1. We want to respond to every animal's needs.

> *What pains me the most is being unable to give the animals what I think they need, e.g. enough personal one-on-one time, a more calm environment, enough walks and play time, etc.*

In other words, that wonderful individual bonding with any animal under your care also sets you up for frustration in satisfying this desire to help all of them. After feeling firsthand each animal's unique, loving interactions with us, we want every animal friend we meet or hear about to have that same chance to bond with their very own human. The physical, mental, emotional, and soulful connections that we experience are grounded in reality. It only takes one relationship with one animal for each of us to realize the potential in all of them. As simply stated by one rescuer, "I always want to take every one home." These real, personal experiences strengthen our drive to help people and pets get together and stay together. They also, however, create frustration and sadness when we see animals without that same quality of life we insist on giving to those who are under our care. Often it is these first hands-on experiences with the animals—perhaps our own family pets when we are children—that first ignite that desire to go beyond our own animal family and help even more animals. We experience the gifts of the bond as we watch our pet fully embrace their own joys of being alive, cared for, and loved. We want them all to have those same opportunities at love and family. But at some point, we learn that this may not yet be realistic.

> *I feel the animal has completely entrusted himself to me and it is my responsibility to never let him down and that is not always possible.*

2. Rescue is an exhilarating, addicting, and haunting process.

> *Sometimes, during an emergency or disaster, you see one hundred things that need to get done and you physically can only do twenty. The feeling of disappointment weighs down on you and you tell yourself you should have worked harder, stayed up longer, and maybe slept less or taken a shorter break, and then maybe you could have gotten more done.*

In the midst of a crisis, animal advocates who are in rescue mode shift their gears into "full steam ahead." They cannot prioritize such matters of the heart; every animal deserves to be saved, and it only takes one successful rescue to bring indescribable elation to the advocates involved. It's real life at its best! At the same time, however, it also brings the acute awareness of all the other animals in need—every hour of every day. Furthermore, realism tells us that the relief we may have just given to one animal may not be available for another. Animal rescue volunteers who I counseled after Hurricane Katrina described their rollercoaster of emotions—the extreme joy followed by tremendous anguish—while working against time to save the stranded pets. After bringing one needy pet to safety, their sense of fulfillment was quickly replaced with the aching feeling that time was running out for the others who were equally deserving of being saved.

3. There are overwhelming needs with limited resources.

> *What pains me is not having enough homes for all the animals.*

The statistics of real life tell us that our vision for the animals has not yet been achieved. But we can rejoice in the progress that has been made when we see the real life numbers that indicate more animals are being saved every year. We see the widespread growth of more organizations dedicated to improving the lives of our furry friends. However, as strides are being made in one area of animal welfare, new needs are presented. Modern technology gives us information and images of animals around the world in all facets of life that are being saved as well as those that continue to live in deplorable conditions. The effects of this knowledge are reflected in one advocate's statement: "I often feel overwhelmed with requests for help. Will there ever be a time when there aren't so many animals in need? Not when I am told there are 400 million stray animals worldwide (give or take another hundred million)." When we compare what we want for all animals everywhere to what their lives currently are it is realistically endless work! A woman dedicated to feral cat trap, neuter, and return notes, "By the end of winter, I start thinking that we really are making progress getting all the feral cat colonies managed—spayed and neutered. Then when spring hits and the enormous number of pregnant cats and newborns start coming I wonder if we have really made any progress at all! This happens every year!"

4. We face the "front lines."

> *We are the ones in the trenches with no financial support holding our finger in the dike.*

The "front lines," as defined by Faith, refers to being in the position where you are directly hit with or witness to the requests for helping animals in need. On the positive side of this reality, there is indescribable satisfaction in taking a previously abused animal into your arms to safety. But then there is also the angst and despair one can feel being on the other end of the phone listening to a story about an animal in need and struggling with the need to say no and the desire to say yes. Animal advocates working the front lines describe the most stressful aspects of being right there:

> *The people whose lack of care results in the sad fate the animals face.*
>
> *The neglect, abuse, pain, and suffering in the animal kingdom worldwide.*
>
> *The walk-ins and daily calls I hear of animals in distress.*
>
> *An animal right in front of me that I cannot help.*

SENSITIVITY

It is in the animal advocate's nature to experience intense feelings for animals. Empathy, compassion, and love readily flow in their presence. I have identified four factors that make up this natural ability to emotionally connect:

1. We have strong empathy and concern for animals.

> *One of the worst parts of trapping a feral cat for me is when the trap door slams shut . . . those first few seconds tear my heart apart. One can only imagine how terrified the poor animal is those first few seconds. It's agonizing to watch and always makes me cry.*

We feel what we think they feel. It's not "just an animal." We read the pain in their eyes, we interpret their whines and barks and meows. We feel their excitement and we imagine their disappointment. One animal sanctuary caregiver explained, "Feeling a dog's boredom, frustration, and anxiety and not being able to do anything to change it is hardest for me to handle."

> *Seeing unhappy animals is always hard. . . . I can still see the sadness in their eyes.*

2. We have a natural ability to receive love from and bond with the animal (even by only hearing about one in need).

> *It's the ones that suffer unknown that I worry about at night.*

There is nothing so soul-touching as connecting with one of our beloved furry friends. Animal advocates agree that nothing compares to the unique meaning and joy it brings to life. One advocate remarks, "They are my healthiest relationships! I can't imagine not having dogs and cats in my life." We have truly been blessed with the ability to connect with animals in a unique way. Most people who care deeply for the animals have either felt this way for as long as they can remember, or have had a certain "trigger" event that awakened their souls. Childhood memories reported by animal lovers include being unable to watch movies or read books where animals are suffering or dying, and preferring stuffed animals to dolls. The love for animals, and the desire to be around them often begins at an early age after one experiences their immense charm, and the pleasure of being in their presence. My sister and I rescued stuffed dogs at the local thrift store. We begged our mother to let us take them all so one would not feel left behind. Looking back, this was certainly a sign of things to come for me! I have also talked with advocates who did not grow up with pets. Many report that it was their first experience rescuing a dog or a cat that awakened their compelling love and compassion for animals. Whether this empathy reveals itself in childhood, or is triggered later as an adult, it only takes one experience to know when one's sensitivity to animals is evoked; it can never go back to being anything else. And this deep concern for animals reaches far beyond the advocate's own home. Bonding happens over the Internet, digitally, from hearing a story, or that glance of the soulful eyes in a picture. A volunteer photographer described her emotional connection with animals she hoped to help find homes:

> *After spending time photographing and editing and uploading pictures, I developed a bond with those animals and it was very hard to find out that some did not end up in a home.*

That sensitivity brings pain when we empathize with their suffering and intensifies our sadness in times of loss, but it is also a source of great meaning and joy for us

3. Our sense of purpose comes from helping animals.

> *Whatever the work is in support of animals . . . it is abundantly privileged.*

Animal lovers know they will most likely share their journey with these wonderful living beings for the rest of their lives. Although it may be short-lived, helping just one animal in need matters and offers an immediate sense of fulfillment. The dedication to their wellbeing comes naturally to advocates and they often describe their work as being what they were meant to do. It is who they are. One advocate states, "I was born to help animals and I hope to continue this pursuit 'til the day I die." Others say, "I feel responsible to help animals because they are such innocent victims," and "It simply must be done."

4. There is a natural alliance that exists among people who love animals.

> *Sharing the joys and sorrows with others is such a needed reminder that we are not alone.*

We have all had the experience of connecting with others who also feel strongly about the plight of animals. The beginning of a casual statement, "This is my rescued dog . . ." can lead to an intense and lengthy conversation where two animal advocates find they have a lot in common. Ask a question about a furry family member with like-minded strangers and conversation flows. Shared love and concern for animals is an inherent part of the sensitivity component of all animal advocates. While it can serve as a powerful connector for humans, I believe the potential of this aspect has barely been tapped. When such a connection is allowed to happen, its capacity to heal and unite us is vast. As a facilitator of a pet loss support group in Chicago, I have seen that some of the most powerful healing takes place from the fall of an understanding tear or a gentle word of comfort from the other grieving hearts that are present. Participants coming to the support group for the first time commonly express how helpful it was to be with people who truly understood their sorrow.

Think about your IRS. You may choose to write a line about each component as it relates to you and your life:

Idealism (your dreams and beliefs)

Realism (your real-life experiences)

Sensitivity (your empathy for animals)

With a new understanding of who you are as an animal advocate, let's look at the inevitable struggles that may interfere with your ability to fully experience the joy and fulfillment that your unique and purposeful journey with animals offers.

CHAPTER II
THE INEVITABLE CHALLENGES

THE ROLLERCOASTER RIDE

I have heard many animal lovers describe their journey with animals as a rollercoaster ride because of the ups and downs from one moment to the next. It is the conflicting feelings within each component of the IRS that cause the highs and lows when we come face to face with the challenge of wanting more for the animals than we have the capacity to give. For example, when I casually asked one workshop attendee how she was doing she fervently explained that had she answered one hour earlier, she would have said that she was in the depths of despair, but since then, events unfolded surprisingly well for the animal for whom she was particularly concerned and at the moment she was overjoyed. Understanding this dual nature of our IRS gives us a chance to step back and observe how powerful our thoughts can be in obstructing the natural joy underlying the journey. Somewhere along the way our minds turn positive natural desires into nagging thoughts, fears, and unrealistic expectations that we place on ourselves and others.

THE BLOCKING BELIEFS

I have observed three self-depleting beliefs that block the joy of our journey. Each corresponds to one of the three parts of the animal lover's IRS. I call them the "Three Toos":

> **Too Much**: Progress feels too slow, so we expect too much from ourselves and others. (Idealism)
>
> **Too Many**: There are too many to help, so we must keep doing it all. (Realism)
>
> **Too Painful**: It is too painful, so we cannot feel joy. (Sensitivity)

Although these beliefs are formed from the way we view our real life experiences, it does not make them true. Committing to them interferes with our ability to receive the gifts that each day offers for replenishment. We miss the joy. We live in sacrifice and dwell on feelings of ineffectiveness. Whether we call it stress, burnout, or self-sacrifice, or simply being overwhelmed and suffering from compassion fatigue, they are all conditions created by our thoughts and feelings about not being able to do enough. These thoughts drain our energy and push us to go beyond what we can comfortably manage. When we take on more than we are able we become exhausted. Tired and drained, we are unable to feel the joy or receive the gifts of our giving. Without joy, we are depleted. Depleted, we can't find joy, and the cycle continues to spiral out of control. Let's take a closer look at the "Three Toos":

1. Progress feels too slow, so we expect too much from ourselves and others. The same ideals that fuel our passion produce disillusionment when our happy endings do not occur. Disillusionment hits hard when we are faced with the realization that our animal friends are not getting the chances we are fighting for—and that they so deserve. Of course we want our vision to be realized, right now. I remember one of my first experiences volunteering at an animal shelter over twenty years ago. Viewing the organization through my idealistic-colored glasses, I thought the place was magical because dogs and cats were being adopted out at phenomenal rates. I remember the emotional devastation I felt when I realized it was euthanasia, not happy endings that left the kennels empty when I returned in the morning to help. When animal advocates were asked to describe the source of their stress in their everyday lives, disillusionment with the public, with one another, and ultimately with themselves were commonly reported. Examples include the following statements:

> *It is taking us too long to fix the problem. I want to see the end of population control killing in my lifetime, and now that I'm in my fifties, it's harder to keep the faith.*

> *The feeling that we are kidding ourselves and that the measures of success we celebrate are more fantasy than true indicators of societal change.*

We feel discouraged both by what we are not able to do and what others are not doing. We are discouraged with what we cannot do so we have trouble giving ourselves credit for what we do. One advocate cited her biggest stressor as "the slow progress that is seen in the animal world." Another described feeling "the inability to affect change." So it only follows that with too much to do, combined with the perception of sluggish progress toward where we want to be, the animal advocate complains that there are too few to help. This frustration fuels negative feelings toward both the general public who disappoint us and others whose lives are also dedicated to helping animals, but who are not doing enough or helping in the right way. Disillusionment with pet owners and the public are expressed by advocates:

> *Lack of care results in the sad fate the animals face.*

> *My burnout comes from . . . the tremendous lack of support throughout the community.*

> *It's the humans who are the villains in every dog's story.*

> *What causes me the most pain and stress is that literally day by day the American public never ceases to amaze me—their lack of caring about the way our animals are treated is sickening.*

> *I get so emotionally drained by all the thoughts of how uncompassionate, careless, and just downright cruel people can be.*

Disillusionment with fellow animal advocates is also expressed:

> *Even though people who work in the animal welfare movement have the same goal, their way of meeting those goals are extremely different and conflicting. This takes away from some of the hope I have that our goals will ever be met.*

> *I struggle with the knowledge that animal welfare groups have so much difficulty trusting and cooperating with each other. If we can't work together, it's going to take so much longer to stop the killing.*

Advocates expressed frustration in the conflicts that occur within and between organizations that get in the way of achieving the shared goals. Some of these perceptions that block progress are the following:

> *There is an unwillingness of people to try something new or different to achieve the same result.*
>
> *Dealing with the infighting, territoriality, and egos among folks who are supposed to be working toward the same basic goals is frustrating.*
>
> *Some people are not pulling their share of the workload.*

2. There are too many to help, so we try to do it all. Those same hands-on kind of experiences that often bring the adrenaline rush, joy, and sense of success bring us face to face with situations that cause us anger, guilt, and a sense of ineffectiveness.

> *All of us in this field are in a constant uphill battle.*

It's hard to compromise in what we want for all of our animal friends—each and every one of them deserves the best life. The nagging desire to do more is evident in the animal advocates' answers to the following question: What causes stress in your work?

> *Not being able to help as many as I would like.*
>
> *The overwhelming feeling that there is so much need out there!*

> *Not having the time in the day to do all I want for the animals.*
>
> *Working too long and too hard without making myself take a break.*
>
> *Situations keep coming up. Too much!*
>
> *Dealing with the overworked stress of trying to help and care for as many animals as possible while balancing the many obligations of one's day.*
>
> *My own tendency to take on too many; I always figure I can make room for that one.*

It never feels like we have done enough. With too much to do, too many to help, it's too hard to say no so too often we say yes!

3. It is too painful, so we cannot feel the joy. The same natural ability to bond and empathize with the animals that brings warmth, peace, and comfort can also result in feelings of grief, loss, and sadness. Animal advocates sometime experience signs of trauma, including haunting images and nightmares from some of the difficult situations they face. The emotional pain stays with them, as evidenced by statements from animal rescue workers like the following: *I am haunted everyday knowing that there are animals suffering.*

Our thoughts and feelings about what we are not able to do get in the way of the natural joy surrounding our lives with animals. Burdened with the thoughts that progress is too slow, there are too many to help, and it's too painful to bear, what recourse does the animal advocate have? To best answer this question, let me take you back a few years.

When you were a child do you remember the first

few times that YOU were allowed to choose how much of a special treat to put on your plate and you piled on more than you could eat? I remember the first time I was given the chance to create my own ice cream sundae. I started with two large scoops of ice cream and added hot fudge, pecans, caramel, whipped cream, and many cherries on top. I dug in. Halfway through the delicious dessert, however, I felt stuffed. Aware of the "clean your plate " rule in our home, I was relieved when my mother, with an understanding smile, said, "Looks like somebody's s eyes were bigger than her stomach."

Similar to this childhood experience of thinking that we want to eat more than our bodies can hold, we still take on too much. Our desire to help our animal friends is greater than our capacity to do so. Our hearts are larger than our hands. A personal incident illustrates what happens when we ignore the size of our physical capabilities and listen only to our heart's desires. I was one of two people carrying a seventy-five-pound foster dog who had just undergone ligament surgery. At the time, I knew that I was straining my back as I carried the dog in a blanket up the hill through the backyard of the foster home, but I also knew that there was nobody else around to help. It was getting dark, there was a light snowfall that was fast becoming a Chicago blizzard, and the dog was whimpering. I saw no other safe option than to persevere until we eventually reached the back door. Later that night I landed in bed with a sore back and spent the next three days on a heating pad, during which time I could help no animals at all. My heart's desire for the dog was larger than my hands could physically hold.

Besides physically overtaxing ourselves, we animal lovers can also become mentally and emotionally depleted when we try to do more than we can comfortably handle. Feeling overwhelmed, distressed, and depleted, we inadvertently block the joy and sense of fulfillment that our lives with animals naturally hold. We become vulnerable to anxiety and depression, and ultimately to conditions commonly referred to as burnout and compassion fatigue. Personal and family life may suffer, and sometimes we even lose the ability to continue to help animals at all. We are no longer open to receiving all the gifts that our unique journey with animals offers.

Take a moment to look within yourself. How do you feel today? Are you fully experiencing the joy, that is, the contentment and peace of mind that your life's journey with animals offers? Or could you be on the road to depletion, depriving your soul of its vitality and its ability to keep you at your best in all of your interactions with the animals, others, and the world? It's not always easy to know when you are functioning from a state of self-care deprivation. Even my training as a psychologist did not stop me from suffering from emotional and soulful depletion, which I explained away by telling myself that a sacrificial, miserable life was a necessary price to pay when loving and helping animals.

So let's begin within. Take the following self-inventory, *Is Your Heart Larger Than Your Hands*?, to see how the size of your heart, compared to your hands, may be keeping you from experiencing the full joy of your journey.

Is Your Heart Larger Than Your Hands? is divided into two parts. The first part looks at your innermost self. Are the desires that you have to help animals overflowing? People who love animals differ regarding which animals are included in their circle of care and concern. Some animal lovers may be solely focused on their immediate furry family, while others may include the pets they are responsible for in foster care, or at an animal shelter or veterinary clinic in which they work or volunteer. For others, the desire to help expands to those homeless or abused, in the wild, in research labs, or in factory farms. The second part looks at the hands. Are you overloading your physical, mental, and emotional capacity to help the animals? Interpretations provided for this inventory are designed to give you an understanding of your heart's desires in relation to your hands' capacity when it comes to loving and helping animals.

Is Your Heart Larger Than Your Hands?

PART I

Directions: Circle the number "1" to indicate that you never feel that way, circle "2" for seldom, circle "3" for sometimes, circle "4" for usually, and circle "5" for always. Circle "0" if you feel that the statement does not apply to you.

Is your heart overflowing? Regarding your desires to help the animals . . .

DNA	Never	Seldom	Sometimes	Usually	Always
0	1	2	3	4	5

How often do you feel that you:

Would like to do more for your own animals?

0 1 2 3 4 5

Would like to do more for the animals under your care?

0 1 2 3 4 5

Would like to do more to help
companion animals in need?

0 1 2 3 4 5

Would like to do more to help
other animals (e.g. farm/wildlife)?

0 1 2 3 4 5

Would like to do more to educate
people about the issues?

0 1 2 3 4 5

Would like to make more of a
difference for animals?

0 1 2 3 4 5

Would like to do more to change
society's regard for animals?

0 1 2 3 4 5

Are thinking about animals
and what else you could
do to help?

0 1 2 3 4 5

Add up your total points: ___________

Interpretation of Scores

0-9 Scores in this range reflect persons not as involved with animals.
10-25 Scores in this range reflect individuals who love animals, but are able to limit the thoughts and energy given to animals in their lives and focus on one or two specific ways to be involved.
25-32 Scores in this range reflect a person who has strong concerns about animals and actively desires to make a difference in their lives. This range of scores may also reflect animal lovers who are trying to handle their emotions, balancing idealism with realism.
32-45 Scores in this range reflect persons who are highly sensitive to all animals and feel compelled to help them. This drive is a dominant force in their lives; they think about animals every day. Helping animals is a top priority and a major part of their lives.

PART II

Directions: Circle the number "1" to indicate that you never feel that way, circle "2" for seldom, circle "3" for sometimes, circle "4" for usually, and circle "5" for always. Circle "0" if you feel that the statement does not apply to you.

Are your hands overloaded? Regarding your life with animals . . .

DNA	Never	Seldom	Sometimes	Usually	Always
0	1	2	3	4	5

How often do you feel:

Always tired?

0 1 2 3 4 5

There's too much to do?

0 1 2 3 4 5

You are not doing enough?

0 1 2 3 4 5

There's too much information
that comes your way?

0 1 2 3 4 5

Frustrated?

0 1 2 3 4 5

Overanxious about what might happen?

0 1 2 3 4 5

That your life is out of balance?

0 1 2 3 4 5

Overwhelmed by daily responsibilities?

0 1 2 3 4 5

Add up your total points: ___________

Interpretation of Scores

0-16 Individuals who score in this range have no or very little animal-related stress in their lives.

17-24 Individuals with scores in this range are likely to have found coping skills and a realistic perspective in their life with animals that is working for them.

25-31 Individuals with scores in this range are likely to be experiencing a rollercoaster of emotions—ups and downs— feeling overwhelmed on some days and joy and effectiveness on other days.

32-45 Individuals with scores in this range are consumed with feelings and activities regarding their concerns for the animals and desire to make their lives better. They are overlooking their own self-care. The stress feels unmanageable at times and is interfering with other areas of their lives.

OVERTAXED BODY, OVERWHELMED MIND, AND UNDERNOURISHED SOUL

How does having a *heart larger than your hands* affect your everyday life? People show signs of stress differently. The following chart displays some of the common symptoms of inadequate self-care, which can affect a person's wellbeing physically (the body), mentally (thoughts and feelings), and soulfully (sense of aliveness and connection).

Signs

BODY	MIND	SOUL
Constant tension	Crabby, hot-tempered	No pleasure
Head & stomach aches	Anxiety & fears	Looking for escapes
Trouble sleeping	Negativity & dread	Effects on family
Exhaustion	Crying, sadness, panic	Gambling, smoking
Hard to get up	Feeling ineffective	Drinking, addictions
Aches for no reason	Foggy & forgetful	Over & under-eating
More prone to illness	Making more mistakes	Feeling fragile
Takes longer to get well	More critical of others	General distrust

The following statements from animal lovers describe the toll that this depletion takes on their body, mind, and soul. It is easy to see how such thoughts obstruct the innate joy of the journey.

PHYSICAL

I have trouble balancing their physical and emotional needs with mine.

Taking care of all the dogs was overwhelming for me. I was often sick.

Every time I leave the shelter, I am exhausted.

I do not have enough hours in the day to do all the work that needs to be done, I sometimes wish I didn't require sleep.

MENTAL/EMOTIONAL

I feel helpless and frustrated.

I experience a high level of emotional distress much of the time.

Those instances when you cannot follow through with your promise to the animal and that stress builds up and emotionally you begin feeling destroyed.

When I'm not working, I feel like I should be.

I am stressed and overwhelmed mentally, emotionally, and physically when there are insufficient resources to meet the needs of animals I am responsible for.

SOUL

The overall insanity of it all brings daily stress.

I sometimes briefly wish I wasn't working with animals so I wouldn't hear about all the bad stuff.

I overextend myself.

Often, after feeling so depleted, animal advocates want to leave the field. Sometimes they secretly wish they had never stepped foot in it. There is a feeling of being emotionally trapped—wanting to quit what they are doing, but seeing no way out. While they do not want to abandon their sense of purpose, their confidence in being able to get through another day often feels questionable. I have counseled individuals who, while not actively suicidal, believed that peace of mind was not possible while still alive in this world.

EXTENDED EFFECTS OF THE IRS

In addition to the toll these beliefs and behaviors take on us individually and within our world of helping animals, it can also find its way into the rest of our lives, including our relationships with family, friends, and even our beloved animal companions. The following statements are from animal advocates describing the way their feelings of depletion impact their lives:

My personal animals seem to get what's left energy-wise; there's the guilt involved with that.

> *We have lived an abnormal life with the cats coming first. My marriage has suffered and my health has been greatly jeopardized.*
>
> *I have no other personal life left.*

I have counseled couples with broken marriages where one or both spouses have cited the stress of animal rescue impacting their lives. I remember one husband in my office blurting out, "I cannot take one more kitten in the bathtub!" Children of animal advocates often report that while they admire their animal-loving parent, they resent the time that is taken away from them. Mothers and fathers have described to me the guilt and inadequacy they often feel when they choose to respond to an animal emergency knowing they are disappointing their child who was counting on them to participate in some other activity.

While I do not have any children, I felt the effects of my overloaded day-to-day life on my own animal companions. I remember receiving a call that two cats needed to be picked up as soon as possible. The owner was being taken to the hospital and the visiting nurse in charge suggested the two indoor-only, declawed cats be let out to take care of themselves. As I was quickly getting ready to pick up the cats to put them in foster care, I remember feeling frantic and yelling at my own older, arthritic dog to hurry up and come inside. On another occasion, a friend of mine gently suggested that the best thing I could do for my blind and disabled dog would be to find a way to reduce my own stress and tension.

ISOLATING EFFECTS OF THE "THREE TOOS"

In addition to blocking the joy of the journey, depleting beliefs and actions of the well-intended IRS cause conflicts among and between animal advocates. Overwrought with frustration, it is easy to find fault with others who are not doing enough; the IRS is relentless and prepared to fight rather than let the animals down. This uncompromising stance and misdirected energy not only compromises the effectiveness of the individuals, the groups, and the overall progress of changing the lives of animals, it unintentionally discourages others from joining the cause. Sadly, we lose just what we need to make our lives and those of animals better: potential new supporters and the camaraderie of others who share in our vision.

So how does this happen? Why is it so easy for like-minded animal advocates to clash with each other? A closer look at the IRS provides the answer to this question. When faced with conflict, each of its three components attempts to employ a giving strategy that requires others to behave in an expected way. Not only does this approach fail to lead to a resolution, it produces anger, frustration, and disappointment that fuel the division that occurs among the very animal advocates who could be working together and supporting each other. Separation leads us farther away from being at our collective best to attain our vision for the animals.

Let's take another look at the idealist. The drive to attain a certain vision creates what I call a *controller*. This happens when the idealist, previously motivated by passion and then discouraged by disillusionment, decides to force change. In other words, it resolves to take control. Since the vision has not been realized the way things have been going, the idealist determines that it is time to demand change. A plan that others are expected to follow is set in motion. For example, one group may decide that more stringent adoption requirements will prevent pets from being returned by owners. Another group takes control of the increase in shelter admissions by
deciding to relax the criteria for adopters. Expecting others

to follow their lead, it is clear to see how conflict within and between groups occurs when the idealistic controller attempts to take charge. Anger and frustration can now be directed at the inadequate owners and the "wrong policies" of the rescue groups. Becoming judgmental of the differing views of others, they become demanding and difficult to work with. A sense of ineffectiveness ensues in the *controller* as unproductive and exhausting energy is spent attempting to change others.

How does the realism component of the IRS attempt to reach its goal of helping all the animals in need? It creates and demands unrealistic expectations by becoming what I call a *trader*, that is, a giver who attempts to force change by expecting others to give to the same degree that they do. For example, a faltering organization may decide that all volunteers must give an extra five hours a week to the cause. Or one rescue group expects the other to be able to take the same number of pets in an emergency situation, and they expect donations for the cause to be equally distributed according to the number of pets rescued. When things are not as equitable as expected, individuals and groups again become the target for the anger and frustration in not being able to save all the animals. The realist, as a *trader,* expects rewards to match the sacrifice. For example, the *trader* expects that if she is willing to give up her vacation to trap feral cats, then others should be at least willing to manage the colony. When this doesn't happen the *trader,* who was most likely in desperate need of a vacation, feels cheated, angry, and betrayed. When I was facilitating an online forum on managing emotions in animal rescue the following question was posed: What was the key to get other volunteers to put in the same effort, time, and sacrifice that one volunteer did? Like the idealistic *controller*, the realistic *trader* identifies the uncooperative and unfair people as the barrier to the changes they want for the animals.

Finally, the sensitivity aspect of the IRS takes

action that only leads to stressed giving. Disappointment and discouragement turn inward, placing all of the expectation for change on the individual who becomes what I call a *martyr*. The sensitive *martyrs* feel ineffective and present themselves as unhappy, exhausted, and continually self-sacrificing. They operate under the false notion that the degree of personal misery measures one's conviction to the cause. In reality, their gloom and despair turn off others who might consider joining the cause. This ultimately leads to the *martyr's* own depletion.

The strategies created by the thoughts and beliefs of the IRS only lead us further into our feelings of disillusionment and despair. We continue on a path that only depletes—while at the same time turns off others to the idea of joining us—isolating us from the very people we need on our side to truly help more animals. The intuitive wisdom of our soul gets buried deeper and deeper under piles of thoughts and hurt and worries. Joy is trapped under feelings of guilt and sadness. Support from others is hidden behind pride and judgment and a false sense of standing up for the animals. When we use the methods that the three components of the IRS demand, we let our hearts overtax our hands. We let our desire to help animals get in the way of recognizing and meeting our own needs. Changing the isolating effects of the IRS can only begin within an individual's own self. Are you ready to consider balancing your needs with the desires you have to help animals? What thoughts can you change so that your acts of giving to and from the heart can flow naturally again?

CHAPTER III
AWAKENING THE JOY

Until one has loved an animal, a part of one's soul remains unawakened.

- Anatole France

Now that we understand the challenges that we all face together as persons committed to helping animals, how do we move forward in joy? Let's look at the unique and life-enriching journey that awaits us and so naturally bestows joy, love, peace of mind, and fulfillment in our everyday experiences with the animals.

The above statement credited by French poet Anatole France is well known by many animal lovers and is often found on animal welfare organizations' websites and walls. The stirring of the soul, which is our deepest essence, reaffirms to us that there is no turning back on the decision to keep animals in our lives, and no turning back on our passion to give them their best possible lives with us. We have embarked on a path of the deepest kind: a journey of the soul, a life path that unfolds when living every day from your unique sense of self and purpose.

So what does that mean? While the word "soul" is difficult to define, it is commonly thought of as one's deepest essence, the place where one feels most alive. In his book *Care of the Soul*, author Thomas Moore describes the soul as "a quality or dimension of experiencing life and ourselves . . . depth, value, relatedness heart, and personal substance" (Page 6). Soul is both a personal essence deep within, as well as something outside of ourselves. Soul is the place where both your innermost desires and your sense of connectedness to all of life lies. Albert Schweitzer, an animal advocate born a century ago, acknowledges this dual nature of soul when he describes it as "the sense of something higher than ourselves; something that stirs in us thoughts, hopes, and aspirations which go out to the world." Doesn't that describe your everyday life with animals? Experiences with them are felt deeply within, while expanding infinitely out and beyond.

I recently felt this paradox of the soul as I sat on the floor of a veterinary hospital with my brother and sister-in-law as they said their final goodbyes to Cosmo, their beloved family dog for the past fourteen years. Love and aliveness enveloped the room as their adult children called and expressed their love through a cellphone held up to the big yellow lab's ear. The images of that soulful moment now blur together: hugs and kisses, hands and paws, gentle strokes, loving eyes from a cancer-ridden body, the veterinarian's words, and a room full of tears. While I felt the awakening of old pain from my own past losses in years gone by, treasured family memories and immense love for and from Cosmo also flooded the room. Gratitude for the privilege to be present at the end of Cosmo's journey on Earth, along with a feeling of connectedness to my family, the dog, and to all the human-animal companion bonds that have come before and will come after, gave me inner peace and contentment as a previously untouched part of my soul was awakened.

What soul-awakening story comes to mind for you? The soulful journey is compelling. It's second nature for us to have animal friends in our lives and to keep those who are no longer with us alive in our hearts; we cannot resist our urge to give to them and connect with them. The possibilities of a life lived from the soul, our deepest essence, are indescribable. We are sure that you, along with all animal advocates, have felt in your relationships with animals this deep connection that goes beyond words.

Heraclites, a pre-Socratic philosopher, is credited with describing this immeasurable potential of soul when he said, "You would not find out the boundaries of the soul, even by traveling every path, so deep a measure does it have."

So it only follows that a journey directed by the soul would contain both our greatest challenges and our ultimate joys. Let's go back to the definition of joy that Faith and I found best fits the animal advocate's journey: a peaceful contentment that happens when one's deepest desires are honored. In other words, joy is not something to work diligently to achieve. Instead, it is the natural result of giving from the soul, our deepest place. Since helping animals aligns with your life's purpose, you have already experienced the feeling that poet Rabindranath Tagore is credited with having said: "I slept and dreamt that life was joy. I awoke and saw that life was service. I acted and behold, service was joy." These acts of giving bring immeasurable gifts back to the heart, including joy, peace, and a sense of purpose. A poetic verse from Shakespeare's *Merchant of Venice* (act 4, scene 1, vs 180-187) notes the flow to and from the giving heart when he describes the power of mercy as a blessing to the giver as well as the receiver:

The quality of mercy is not strain'd,
It droppeth gentle rain from heaven
Upon the place beneath. It is twice blest:
It blesseth him that gives and him that takes.

As we discussed in the last chapter, to participate in this natural flow of giving to and from the heart, it must be open to receiving the gifts that naturally bring joy and replenishment. We then are able to tap into that natural flow of giving and receiving, which in turn replenishes the joyful heart of the giver.

There are no specific formulas or equations for the amount of time one should spend giving and receiving.

The goal is not even a balanced life. Your days may still be jam-packed with activities that energize and fulfill you, perhaps even exhaust you. A balanced heart is evident by a sense of deep peacefulness that remains even amidst all the challenges you face. Once again, the only place to begin is within. Are you ready? The next chapter offers balancing strategies that we call the Five L's from Linda: look, limit, let go, listen and live.

CHAPTER IV
BALANCING STRATEGY: LOOK

TAKE A NEW LOOK

Let's take a new perspective. Remember the three depleting beliefs about our journey with animals, progress is too slow, there are too many to help, and it is too painful? We can diffuse the power of these joy-stripping thoughts by expanding our outlook on this naturally rewarding life path. A simple change in perception will help us find that balance between our needs and desire to help the animals more easily.

TAKE IT FROM FAITH

I found it a huge shock to come face to face with the daily indifference, neglect, and casual cruelty exhibited toward the dogs, cats, and horses by some of the people I was relating to in my role as unofficial animal control officer at the start of Best Friends back in the 1980s.

It was the first time I had ever seen such horrid behavior toward animals, right before my eyes. I became angry all of the time. My ability to relate to people, except close friends who felt like I did, was shrinking fast, until my world became a very painfully small place to inhabit. I was truly burned out.

My vision became limited. You know how it is when your glasses get dirty and you can only see out of one tiny corner, and even that part is a little smudged? I was living inside my head and seeing only a few blurry, unpleasant slivers of the outside world. My friends and colleagues stepped in when they saw how much pain I was in and helped me step back from that role as unofficial animal control officer. We returned that responsibility to the local law enforcement community after making some improvements, such as helping renovate the existing shelter, and even helping to pay for a civilian to do the job I had been doing.

As I got distance from the day-to-day dealings, something happened in my head. I began to see the community in a different way. Although I was raised in the UK and was a product of a dog-loving Irish family who viewed animals as friends and pets, many of them were the sons and daughters of ranchers or country people used to relying on animals for their livelihoods. To those people, animals were something to be raised for food or to help them work. We were worlds apart in culture, experience, and values. But what they were doing made sense within their worldview.

I still did not like a lot of the way some people were treating their dogs and cats, but I was suddenly able to see it in different context. Just as I could not help how I was raised, neither could they. A new conversation could begin at a place of understanding now that I didn't see them as evil, but just different. The anger lessened. My negative thoughts were replaced by ideas about how to reach out to make the changes needed to help those animals.

That's what seeing any situation from a new perspective can do for us all.

Ellen Gilmore, who brings rescue groups from all over the country together as part of a Best Friends

Network, says the following about becoming narrowly focused on what angers you:

> Our network coalition has come together with an agreed upon purpose: to save lives. I look at the bigger picture. When you live your mission or your goal there is no room for the petty stuff. By staying focused on the goal, and on being positive, you see what can be done. The rest is academic.

Sounds simple. And it is. It's a matter of deciding where you put your eyes.

Look at the Big Picture

This balancing strategy counters the stress-inducing belief often held by our idealistic self that progress feels too slow because we expect too much. This thought is based on our limited experience with only what is directly around us and our need to see life change at a pace that matches our commendable expectations. When we look at the larger picture we can see how everything fits together and is moving at the only pace it can. When we replace expectation with acceptance we can enjoy whatever degree our actions contribute positively to the greater whole of life.

See the Smallness

Realizing our place in this larger picture helps us feel peacefully small. We are able to put our lives into the perspective of a grander scheme. My first thought about this came from a map of the solar system that was hung in a woman's private cat sanctuary. It was a large oblong poster that took up much of one wall and included all the galaxies. Amidst the stars and planets, there was a tiny dot with an arrow pointing to the planet Earth that read YOU ARE HERE. I know when I have felt the weight of the world on my shoulders, the memory of this picture helps me remember that I am only one person in one organization, in one city in one state, in one country, which only resides on one planet in one galaxy. Sure, I will still continue to wholeheartedly do my part to help that one animal inside that small dot on the map where I reside, and each loving act counts, but looking at the bigger picture allows me to realistically feel my lack of control over the universe. I feel this same wonderfully small feeling when I am walking in the canyons in Utah. It brings me peace to know that I am just one of many people who came before and who will continue to come after me with their ideals and contributions to a changing world.

SEE THE LARGENESS

Accepting the bigger picture includes recognizing that we live in an imperfect world. Perhaps acknowledging the flawed world sounds counterintuitive to living from joy and you may wonder how that could possibly be a stress-reducing strategy. The value of taking this view allows our challenges to be put into a realistic perspective.

We realize that we are intelligent and caring human beings so there will always be conditions in the world that we want to change. Simply being alive in this world means we will see there are many areas where compassionate care, creativity, and hard work are needed.

As advocates, we are choosing to put our energy in helping to improve the lives of animals. Disillusionment and disappointments, however, are not only reserved for animal advocates, but are experienced by anyone driven by compassion as they devote themselves to making things better in a flawed world.

There is a cartoon I like that I saw posted on a friend's refrigerator. It shows a man despairingly asking God why he doesn't do anything about all the sadness in the world. The cartoon shows God's reply being, "But I did . . . I sent you." There are many needs and we are willing to put our efforts into areas of life that we believe are most aligned with our purpose. We are each only one person willing to tackle just a few of the many areas of need in one part of the universe. No matter how hard we try or the depth of the sacrifices we make, it will never be enough to achieve our desired vision of the world. All acts of kindness matter and make a difference, but we share this responsibility with billions of others. The sooner we recognize our true size, the easier it is to live within our limits and accept them.

SEE THE RELATIVITY

Accepting the bigger picture also brings our focus to the time we live in now as it relates to the past and future. Consider this time that you are alive on Earth from a historical perspective. Changing the world is an admirable ongoing project that has been part of the lives of many generations before us and will continue to be for many that will follow. Just in the past twenty-five years since I have been actively involved in the movement to better the lives of animals, society has come a long way in its outlook. The majority of pet owners now view their dogs and cats as family members. Animal shelters, foster-based rescue groups, spay-neuter organizations, and humane education initiatives have multiplied by the thousands and have changed the way that people view their pets. There is an increased awareness of the need to ensure wildlife and farm animals are treated humanely. Modern (social) media connects animal advocates all over the world, contributing to both feelings of distress when we hear about animals we cannot help as well as feelings of elation when our connections contribute to a life saved. This is the time in history that we were born into, in which we were meant to live and share our gifts. Each of our efforts grows the movement to help animals. It is a movement in progress. We are pioneers in an ever-growing evolution toward the creation of a kinder world for all living beings.

Look at the Greater Vision

We can counter the depleting thought that there are too many to help so we must keep doing it all by expanding our vision of who is included in our team of people who help the animals. We did not personally create the problems for the animals that we feel so driven to help solve, yet we are committed to working toward being part of the solution. We can and should encourage every individual to do his or her part, not just the animal advocates. Let's go ahead and put a challenge out there to all people who are in the community and to the greater society at large: take a new look. Can we work toward the ultimate vision of a societal shift where it is a natural occurrence for everyone to involve themselves as needed? What if more individuals considered the following words credited to Native American Chief Seattle in an 1854 speech when he asked, "What is man without the beasts? If all the beasts were gone, man would die from a great loneliness of spirit. For whatever happens to the beasts, soon happens to man. All things are connected." We continue to work toward the vision of a society with the guiding principle that we need to create a kinder world for all living beings. With everyone doing their part, there will not be too much to do for any one advocate for animals.

SEE A NEW ROLE

What if taking a new look meant that instead of modeling a life of depletion and sacrifice we were able to be healthy and joyful role models for others? By presenting ourselves as well-balanced and happy individuals united by a common passion and energized by the rewards of giving to animals, we will attract others to our cause. And ultimately, building our collective force will increase the speed at which a greater societal shift has a chance to occur. This means that instead of taking it all on, or even feeling guilty for not doing it all, we realize the value in taking care of ourselves as we "sell" animal advocacy to those who do not as readily embrace the passion. As we take a new look at our call to action, perhaps we can consider, as a top priority, empowering and educating others in order to enhance change. We believe in bringing out the best in all of us.

Looking at the greater vision, we commit to showing that living with compassion for the animals is a positive way to be! We do not want to perpetuate the reputation of the animal person who just does it all—exhausted and resentful, complaining about what others are not doing, or being the talk of the neighborhood for overdoing or over collecting. Rather, we are showing others the wonderful gifts that loving and helping animals offers. So how do we empower, encourage, and energize others? Ask yourself if it is possible to ask the person coming to you for help, to stretch their effort a little, rather than you simply taking full responsibility for the animals in need. Perhaps sometimes we are a little too quick to say yes, to take it all on, thus depriving others who may actually be in a better position to help and thus enjoy the benefits themselves. People may be more willing to do their share more than we think; sometimes they just didn't realize what they might be able to do. Some people mistakenly believe any issue related to an animal needs to be given to an "animal person." For example, I often found there were relatives willing to temporarily take in a pet while the owner was hospitalized. They simply needed to realize the value in saving the bond and to be asked to help. People who find a lost dog or cat are usually more than willing to do the right thing, keeping the pet safe until the family is found, so long as they are given guidance. Individuals faced with the challenge of re-homing a pet can often do it themselves with a few tips on how to put the word out to potential adopters, make a good flyer, and screen potential new homes. They may even be able to find that likely new family more quickly through their circle of friends, neighbors, and coworkers, or perhaps through people who are personally invested in that particular pet's wellbeing.

I learned this lesson firsthand only because I was not able to help a pet walker's urgent request for a cat in need. Had I been available, I would have offered to go get the cat myself and I would have missed the opportunity to empower the pet walker who ultimately became another person helping an animal. Realizing I could not honor her request for help as soon as it was needed, I encouraged her to take action and rescue the cat from the apartment where the owner and the cat were to be evicted by noon. And she did. Not only did she become personally involved with the welfare of this cat, she became a volunteer and supporter for Blessed Bonds.

This unintentional but delightful animal advocate recruitment was not an isolated incident. A friend of mine found a friendly declawed cat in her yard. After consulting with me and exhausting all the ways of finding the cat's possible original family, my friend asked me where she might be able to take the cat so she could be re-homed. After a simple question to her—"Do you think this cat may have come to you for a reason?"—my friend, without hesitation, welcomed the lost cat into her family. Previously, she had used her remarkable animal communicating gifts only to work with dogs, but after this cat became part of her family, she began working with and donating her intuitive skills to helping feline friends as well.

Share an Idea

We can also take advantage of multimedia, and in addition to phone consultations we can easily support others with written, visual, and audio instructions through emails and Internet links. Many rescue groups encourage the people who find kittens in their yards to foster them and they then provide detailed information on bottle feeding, kitten-rearing, and even how to find them permanent homes. While many of us have the tendency to immediately say yes to an animal in need, perhaps we need to step back and realize we are missing the chance to bring another active animal advocate into our realm. We do not want to deprive them of an experience that would help move them along in their own purposeful journey with the animals. In recent years, my ideal vision has been a time when animal shelters are replaced with animal assistance centers where individuals could receive guidance in helping animals and even temporary boarding when necessary. Perhaps there would be volunteers or staff available to educate, check for a microchip, and help create flyers. I would love to see the thought "Give the problem to an 'animal person'" replaced with "What help do I need in order to face the challenge that this animal has presented me with?"

As we look at the greater vision, we are able to let go of the belief that we must take full responsibility for animal requests that come our way. When we hear about an animal or are asked to help it is so easy to feel that we must be the one to take action. We are quick to take it on as if it has always been our responsibility. Many animal advocates have told me that a large portion of the daily anxiety they experience comes from wondering what animal request will come their way and what they will do. It is great that we are often able to step in where others have failed or have dropped the ball, but too often we feel tremendous guilt when we have to say no. We can then remind ourselves that while we may feel compelled to help, we need not view it as our immediate crisis that we must handle alone. We can ask what we might be able to do at that moment. It may be that we can take the animal under our care or we may only be able to give advice and encouragement, or a referral. Again, it's important to remind ourselves that the best way to help may be to empower the person requesting our help. He or she may be in a position to uncover the answer, or find power within his or her own resources.

STAY CONNECTED

Remember to continually look toward all the possible help and support that this greater picture and vision provide. Work together whenever possible. You are just one option for that animal in need. Who else can help you help? Consider all possibilities. Get help from everybody—animal groups, other volunteers, neighbors, or the Internet. You are not alone and you are not the only answer even though sometimes it feels that way. There are other people and organizations that also may be able to help. Perhaps it is not you or your organization that are the best option at that moment that you are being asked. Is educating the person with the request possibly the best option for that pet in need? Love and concern for animals often makes the advocate immediately say yes to situations that will lead them to be overstressed and overloaded. And one of the best things you can do for animal welfare is set an example of helping without becoming that frazzled person.

A LESSON FROM THE BANYAN TREE

The interconnection of all animal advocates can be likened to the incredible banyan tree, a vibrantly growing tree that expands, one trunk at a time, to what has been described as a forest. Although it starts as a single trunk, it produces aerial roots that plant themselves back into the ground and form new tree trunks. The individual trunks produce their own roots that become their own individual trees while strengthening the original tree by remaining connected to it. With every new growth, not only does each individual trunk become stronger, but the banyan tree becomes its own ever growing, expanding, and awe-inspiring entity. I picture every animal advocate as part of the greater ever growing and expanding movement to help animals—the trunks of the banyan tree. As we receive support from each other, our unique contributions grow and express themselves. While we each do our part, it is our connection to each other that expands and enhances the collective strength of all of us—a continually growing force that is found at the core root of our being.

LOOK WITH ACCEPTANCE

To counter the depleting belief that says there's too much pain so I cannot be happy, try looking with acceptance; that is, allowing life to be as it is. Accept ALL the feelings that your exceptional journey with the animals brings. When you accept what is you open yourself up to the possibility of finding peace of mind even amidst sadness. There is a natural relationship between happiness and sorrow. It only follows that the pleasure we receive from a special bond we have with a pet will turn to sadness when that pet is no longer with us. If you try to avoid the sadness and the challenges, you will also limit your capacity for intense joy and fulfillment. Accepting the fact that pain will exist on your journey of love allows you to more fully appreciate the happy times.

After all—it is a journey of the soul—can we really expect experiences of depth and value and relatedness to happen without also facing sadness, heartache, grief, and loss? Of course not. It comes along with the package. It is about being open to life. It is the nature of living every day from that deep place of the soul where feelings are stirred and love overflows. When you realize it is part of the journey you no longer need to fear the pain, or find it insurmountable, abnormal, or unbearable. It simply is what it is.

Accept the sadness in the context of a rich and heartfelt life. Commit to a happy life that contains sadness, but is not defined by it. We already know that our animal friends have shorter life spans than we do so as intensely wonderful as our lives with them can be, grief and loss is unavoidable because we will outlive them. Guilt, sadness, anger, frustration, feeling overwhelmed, and being discouraged are all part of the journey. Acceptance allows us to have these feelings without allowing the feelings to overwhelm us.

Accept the true meaning of happiness. Are you looking for a life that moves only from one pleasure to another? As far as I know, that's never been achieved. But you can find the kind of true happiness that Helen Keller talked about as happening as a result of "fidelity to a worthy purpose" rather than through "self-gratification." In other words, when we are able to apply our authentic gifts, talents, and motivation to worthy causes that go beyond our own day-to-day pleasures, a happy life naturally emerges.

When you look at life with acceptance, you also choose to look for joy. Find joy. Did you ever look for all of the hidden treasures in the popular children's series *Where's Waldo?* Similarly, ask yourself the question, "Where's the joy?" and find it. It is always there for your discovery—every day. And just like the task of finding Waldo, it may be hidden in the obvious. It sometimes takes a willingness to give life a second look from a different viewpoint to find it.

When facilitating pet loss support groups, I find that simply reminding grieving human companions to continue to find joy in their lives—even while in the midst of their grief—is a powerful help. The person experiencing the loss often feels that it is not possible and should not be possible to laugh and smile during the time that follows the death of a beloved pet. I reassure them that their pets devoted much of their lives to bringing joy to their human family and that they would approve. Think about a pet you have lost. Would your beloved want to be the cause of your unhappiness and depression? Reminiscing about happy times often is a good start to getting through the pain. The joy is always there; you simply need to uncover it. Decide that you are going to choose to be happy. Ask yourself, "Will I be able to help more animals by focusing on the sadness?" Sure, you don't need to deny it—we all know sorrow is there. When we are involved with helping animals we are going to have more of everything in our lives, and thus more inevitable experiences of loss, whether it is an animal's natural death, one we hear about that cannot be saved, or even the feeling of loss as one of the pets under our care is adopted. You can accept these feelings and choose to look to the positive and choose to be happy.

Look Toward the Positive

There are always both positive and negative aspects present in each day and in life in general. While this simple truth is not in your control, choosing where to place your focus is up to you. Think of two types of lenses available to you that you can look through as you see your day: one colors events in a more positive perspective, the other more negative. Which lens are you going to pick up?

Keep Reminders

Keep your happy stories of love, joy, and success handy for you to access at any moment: on your computer desktop, in newsletters, magazines, bulletin boards, and around the lunch table. Accent the positive. Look to the stories of the animals that have been helped and the positive changes that have been made. Keep encouraging stories, positive people, and reminders readily available and present. An attendee of Giving Heart Retreat described her "happy file" on her computer desktop that she can tap into in a moment of need for encouragement. Make it a daily part of your life. When you hear yourself dwelling on a negative—discipline yourself to come up with a positive. My husband and I do this to each other whenever one of us complains about a person or situation. We say, "Now name something positive about the day ahead." To avoid drowning in the negative, we might need to make a conscious effort at times to focus on the good that is still always there. The positivism can spread; it affects how we feel. Forcing positive thoughts may start out as a coping strategy, but then it takes on a life of its own and it is contagious to others.

Look to the positive with pride. Be proud of who you are and what you do. You are allowing natural love inside to express itself. During the annual Giving Heart Retreat facilitated by Faith and me at Best Friends Animal Sanctuary, we include an exercise where each participant gives a statement about what they do that brings them a sense of pride. We start them out with the phrase, "I am proud . . ." Each sentence is written on a flipchart, and then a group poem is created from the collective statements. Sometimes we are struck by the difficulty people have in coming up with their sentences. They are so used to focusing on what they are *not* able to do that it takes a little extra effort to focus on what they *are* able to do. While facilitating a workshop for a Minnesota humane society, the participants had such a difficult time completing the sentence that we were not able to complete the exercise. One advocate remarked that with all there is to do to help the animals, her contribution felt so small that it was hard to feel a sense of pride about any one action. It took a participant's suggestion that we reword the task to finishing a statement that began, "What brings me joy is . . ." This started a reaffirming exchange of positive accomplishments that had helped animals. The following **Proud Moments** were created from a compilation of statements made for this activity at a few of the retreats.

PROUD MOMENTS

We are responsible, loving pet owners.
We are all connected.
We've saved so many lives.
We've shown love to animals that otherwise haven't had any.
We've been a voice for those who cannot speak.
I am not intimidated by people who tell me "They are just animals."
We've helped others understand the value of animals in their lives.
We help spread the word.
Spaying and neutering saves lives.
Every animal counts.
We help regardless of age, health, or behavior.
We help people and pets stay together.
We can be trusted.
We take a stand against cruelty.
We share a common vision.
We're compassionate.
We're changing other people.
We are an unstoppable force.
We're changing the future!

PROUD MOMENTS

I transport homeless animals to safety.
I have received and shared knowledge and experience.
I have assisted others in building cat enclosures.
I have made a difference in the lives of animals I have fostered.
I am proud to be a vegetarian and be part of stopping the killing of animals.
I help animal lovers continue their valuable work.

I have given many animals a forever home and lots of love.
I connect with individual animals and help them be the best they can be.
I help teach people to help themselves and the animals.
I have a giving heart!

Proud Moments

I am proud that I saw a need and I did not turn away.
I stood up for the animals in my community.
I spoke for animals in the wild so others would learn.
I cared for the most innocent among us: a rabbit who could not see.
I cared for a sick horse when others would have denied him a chance.
I watched as screech owls took flight again, all because I cared for them.
When disaster has struck I have been there, reaching out to all in need.
I have helped to keep people and pets together.
I have been careful to watch my boundaries, lest I tire and thus falter.
I am the companion to dogs and sheep and goats.
I care for animals injured, and those that are ill.
The dog that is shy can call me "friend."
Of all these things, I am so humbled, and so very proud.
I am proud that I saw a need and I did not turn away.

Proud Moments

I help people who love animals to continue to do their life-saving work.

I am proud of bringing lots of people into my work with animals,
And I am proud of all the animals that I have a chance to make happy.
I am proud to have finally found my mission in life
Where I help save lives everyday.
I create enrichment projects for my kennel inmates,
And I created a transport program that saved the lives of forty-five dogs,
And I have been able to change the stereotypes of pit bulls in the eyes of others,
And I am proud of all the people I have helped in my casework.

PROUD MOMENTS

I love to help animals and people connect.
I am dedicated to bettering the lives of animals and people.
I help make a difference in getting pets into forever homes.
I am proud to be a foster parent.
I am able to take cats out of terrible situations.
I am proud that hundreds of little kittens call me Mommy.
I am honored and blessed to be able to help animals improve their quality of life.
I have saved many un-savables.
I am proud to bring animals and people together.
I am happy I go into schools and talk to kids about responsible pet ownership.
I am proud to be a human that has opened my heart, home, and energy to animals.

Proud Moments

I am proud of all the dogs for which we found happy homes,
And proud of all the positive people who believe in what we do.
I am proud of learning that I have greater capabilities than I thought I had
And that I have stretched my mind and spirit.
I am proud of hanging in there for over thirty years
And being mom to 536 cats, plus three of my own.
I am proud to make a difference with some of the animals at the sanctuary
And proud that all of my life experiences have helped me do what I love to do—
And that I haven't given up.
Proud that I can help educate the public about parrots and the special conditions that they need.
I am proud of the loving home I have provided for my seven companion animals
Over the last thirty-two years.
I am proud of being in the moment with both my personal and sanctuary dogs.
I am proud to have adopted two lovely horses, saving them from a life of breeding.
I am so proud to be part of this greater work that we collectively share.

Proud Moments

I am proud . . .

Of the TNR I did with the kittens in my backyard.
Being present with owners when their pets are euthanized.
Setting the limit of the animals I take into my home at a healthy limit.

The efforts I've made to help people find lost pets; even the ones we did not find.
Giving dog owners an alternative for the dogs to have a quality of life.
Of changing how people feel about feral cats.
Of being able to take care of sick or dying animals, connecting people to a compassionate vet.
To have helped with the Puppy Mill dogs.
Of the work on the Navajo Reservation with the dogs and the cats.
Of the work with the medically needy dogs and helping them to heal.
Of the healing touch work I do on both the feral and sick cats.
Of the medical skills I have learned to deal with emergencies.

PROUD MOMENTS

I am proud...

Of my compassion.
That we are out in the community more than ever before.
That we are changing the mindset of people-ranchers, etc.
That we are opening their eyes to the decisions they are making.
Of supporting our local shelter that rescued our dog.
Of showing respect for animals that have passed away.
Of my church that holds memorial services to help people grieve their pets.
Of opening my heart for each animal's story.
Of everyone who allows themselves to be open to their vulnerability.
Of my commitment to animals.

This collection of **Proud Moments** certainly shows that there were plenty of actions taken for which all of us can take pride and feel joyful. But when we begin within and challenge the way we see things now, other balancing strategies that uncover the joy in the journey begin to feel within our grasp. So let's take a look at the next one, setting limits.

CHAPTER V
BALANCING STRATEGY: LIMIT

SET LIMITS

As animal advocates, our usual response to any and every animal in need is to help. So at first, setting limits will seem unnatural and even counterintuitive to following your heart's desires. It is a necessary step, however, to being able to continue to give from a replenished heart. Since the idea of putting restrictions on one's good intentions has negative connotations, a positive way of stating this same balancing strategy is to say that you will follow your heart's desires with a disciplined mind, that is, also considering what your heart needs for itself. Just like all of the balancing strategies, setting limits must begin within you. Each advocate needs to find his or her own personal limits and set them. It is only when the individual's boundaries are in place that the groups and organizations can then learn their own limitations and function effectively within those confines.

TAKE IT FROM FAITH

"Don't answer the helpline phone, Faith. You

know you always say yes."

This is what I heard from my friends in those early days of Best Friends back in the 1980s. It didn't help that I was both animal and people responsive. So when I would hear about someone losing their job or having to move to a place that didn't take animals I would get caught up in that dilemma, as well as knowing that now a dog or a cat, or any animal for that matter, was also in need of help.

Any no-kill sanctuary has only so much space, and overcrowding leads to terrible consequences for the animals. I wasn't thinking clearly by saying yes to every request that came my way. Saying yes felt good to me, but it wasn't realistic. It was, in a way, downright selfish. The animals already in our care needed a quality life and by not accounting for space requirements or recourses, I put that in jeopardy. So while I thought I was being compassionate, in reality I was being shortsighted, mainly because it made me feel good to say yes.

Self-awareness, knowing what our own strengths and weaknesses are, is a wonderful asset. I am often asked how those of us who started Best Friends survived the turmoil of starting an animal rescue organization and can continue working together and remain friends over thirty years later. Being able to acknowledge strengths and weaknesses in ourselves and in each other is a good part of the answer. It's tough to come face-to-face with personal deficiencies or failure and admit mistakes, but that's where the truth lies. I had to admit that my friends were right. I do not have the natural ability to distance myself from the plight of a person or animal. I was not the right person to answer the phone. Not hearing the stories was a good solution for me, so someone more emotionally suited to that role could step in to answer the phone. I was good at many other things, like taking care of dogs, and passing on knowledge to others through teaching workshops. Those were my skills.

Nancy Ede is a volunteer with Castoff Pet Rescue in Georgia. Nancy used to do a lot of jobs with that organization, anything that was needed, really, including being on the board of directors at one time. Then she stopped trying to do it all. "I work with the cats," Nancy said. "I decided that I need to focus on my passion and my passion is cats—bottle babies, pregnant moms, feral cats, blind cats, cats of any kind that need my help," she said. Nancy had come to this conclusion after having spent ten years working with Deepak Chopra, the renowned physician and spiritual teacher. He talks a lot about finding your passion. She took his advice. "When I am working with cats, that's all I am doing," Nancy told me. "Deepak says, 'Get your mind off yourself,' so that's what I do. Working this way makes it all about the cats, in my case, but it applies across the board." Nancy is using limits not to do less or to restrict her scope of cats that she takes in. In fact, Nancy's house is given over to cats of all kinds, which she and other volunteers take care of. She has limited the species she relates to and other tasks associated with the organization. She does handle her own cat records and the majority of adoptions, but avoids the areas of rescue that would take her away from her passion.

Nancy told me that at the beginning of many of his presentations, Deepak Chopra tells his students to ask themselves these questions: Who am I? What do I want? Neither question is easy to answer, but trying to answer them will take you closer to your passion. Just as Nancy and I found out what we were good at and stopped doing things we were not good at, you, too, can use limits to help you narrow your focus. It might take a few missteps if you get involved with something that does not work for you, but with this knowledge you can pick yourself up and keep trying until you land on your own passion.

Honor Strengths and Weaknesses of Yourself

As you consider setting your limits, begin by assessing your most natural gifts and talents. In other words, how do you give best? What kind of giving flows most naturally for you? An easy way to discover your strengths is to first identify those tasks that feel most difficult and draining for you. The advocate's passion and strong commitment can sometimes mislead them into thinking that they want to do everything possible related to helping animals. It all feels worthwhile to do because all activities related to bettering the lives of animals are invaluable! But since it is not possible for you to do everything that you want to do, it makes more sense to cut back on the time you spend on the activities which deplete you, and engage in those that are most aligned with your natural strengths. Remember, there are many ways to help animals. You do not have to do it all, and you cannot do it all.

Less is More

Setting limits does not necessarily mean doing less. It means restricting your activities to those you enjoy the most and do the best you can with those activities! How can you go wrong if you are putting your gifts to their best use for the animals? I know a woman who is exceptionally talented at taming feral kittens. She has a part of her home set up for this life-saving activity and loves the work! She was also on the fundraising team for a shelter and in her words, she "dragged herself" away from the kittens to attend those meetings. When she decided to take herself off the fundraising team, she discovered that she had the time and energy to take in more kittens and excel in the way of helping that she most enjoyed.

I have also met other volunteers who realized that working directly with the animals at the shelter was too emotionally painful. They found themselves feeling depressed and unable to let go of their worries about the dogs and cats being adopted into good loving homes. They were able to maintain a positive and enthusiastic spirit by working from their computers at home and helping out at fundraising events. When you are asked to help ask yourself the following questions: Can I honor the request in a way that is aligned with my strengths and interests? Am I taking into account my emotional vulnerabilities? Do my current life conditions support a decision to respond at this time? Do I have all that I need to take action? Re-evaluate your role in improving the lives of animals. Or, if you are in the process of choosing how to help, explore the full range of options. Here are a few questions to get you started:

Do you want to have direct animal contact?

If yes, do you prefer working with animals at the shelter, within your own home or business, or in some other capacity?

Do you prefer to create your own contribution or meet an organization's specific need?

Would you prefer to help through being a role model for or educating others rather than through an organization?

Do you want flexible changing hours or a task that is structured and at the same time every week?

If you choose helping without direct animal contact, do you prefer to work at an event, in a shelter, or from your home?

Would you like to work within a team or by yourself?

I have a friend who has walked dogs at his local animal shelter every Wednesday night for over thirty years! He has determined that for him this is the best way and the right amount of time that he can comfortably give to the animals and still approach each walk with enthusiasm and joy. Another friend of mine does no formal volunteering, but makes herself available to the seniors in her neighborhood who occasionally need assistance with their pets. Sometimes she takes a pet to the vet, walks a dog, and has helped care for the cats of an owner who was hospitalized.

Remember that there are many ways to help animals. You do not have to do it all, and you cannot do it all.

PERSONAL STORY

I think of the time I spent with my nephews and nieces when they were growing up. During my weekly visit with them, I would offer to play any game or participate in any activity of their choosing. I thought that would be the most fun for them, even if it were not for me. I remember sometimes constructing items, such as cars, trucks, and entire villages, from hundreds of intricate little pieces. While this is unquestionably a worthwhile activity, it did not interest me much and certainly was not aligned with any natural talents of mine. Then one day I got the idea to play "dogs and cats." We pretended to be all kinds of different dogs and cats and created and played out various scenarios. This game gave me the chance to teach them about being kind to animals. Through our imaginary play, I taught them how to keep pets safe and healthy and happy family members. I especially enjoyed "nap time" when all the imaginary pets found places to cuddle up and relax. My nephews and nieces loved this game and throughout the years—even into their teenage years—they looked forward to this game. Going with my strength helped to create endless fun for all—and they got to know their aunt's passion.

Almost twenty years have passed since my nephews and nieces and I last played "dogs and cats." Just this past Thanksgiving, however, the game was resurrected with my great nephews; they loved it and asked to play the game again and again all weekend long! My now adult nephews and nieces smiled and reminisced about the old days and the enjoyment that they had felt when they played this imaginative game. If I had kept up only playing with them in the ways that they suggested, which was not much fun for me, we all would have missed out on this deeper way of connecting authentically with one another. Setting limits that allow you to give in ways that are aligned with your natural strengths benefit you and others.

Honor Strengths and Weaknesses of Others in a Group

Within groups and organizations, animals are served best when people can be matched to volunteer or job positions that are most aligned with their natural desires and gifts. Individuals and groups become energized and most effective when they tap into the strengths. Within your own group, get to know your own members. What do they need to give their best? What are their strengths and weaknesses? Is it possible to accommodate your fellow animal advocates so that everyone is giving in a way that is most aligned with who they are?

The leaders of the group can model limit setting by creating and taking breaks in a workday. Of course, when it comes to saving animals, there are emergencies and crises that need immediate attention. It is helpful, however, to recognize them as exceptions within a structure that allows for individuals to rest and re-energize when these overextensions happen. For example, perhaps a late-night rescue could be followed by some additional time for self-care the next day. A veterinarian I met in Bali had just taken a position as director of an animal welfare organization. She told me that one of the board members told her it would be best not to take a lunch—the fear was that everybody would then expect to have time out to eat, too. I suggested that she not follow that bit of advice, but to set aside time each day for herself and the entire team of staff and volunteers to have lunch.

TAKE IT FROM FAITH

Setting limits based on one's particular talents, gifts, and preferences not only enhances one's own ability to help, but enhances the group's ability to grow with the idea that individuals at their best are working together as a team. When thinking back on the success of Best Friends, I feel that we naturally did at least one thing right from the very beginning that worked! Because we knew each other well before we began, it was natural for us to set up a division of labor based on each founder's specific strength. We respected each other's territory and stayed out of one another's business, allowing each of us to focus on what we know best. The end result was a lot of individuals working on what best suited them and then coming together as a whole united team.

Ironically, it is setting limits as a group that will allow more work to get done. Rather than harnessing just one individual's enthusiasm and passion to do it all, there are now many people feeling empowered to help in all the different ways that each person has always dreamed a team of people could. They need to find their niche based on the group's mission, and strengths of the individuals involved, and then stay within its boundaries, being the best they can be at what they choose to do. It is also easier for an individual to keep to the limits that they have set for themselves when the agreed upon parameters of the group are firmly in place. For example, if a group decides that their main mission is spay-neutering feral cats, they may put a policy in place that keeps bottle-feeding of newborn kittens off the list of services that they offer. An individual group member presented with such a situation will know to refer to another organization for help rather than taking on the task. It is easier for groups to find ways to work together toward a common goal when clearly defined parameters are presented.

HELPING WITHIN THE LIMITS

I started Blessed Bonds with the mission of providing assistance so that families could keep their pets in times of crisis. I also, however, received many requests from people who simply wanted to re-home their dogs and cats. Although this was not part of the Blessed Bonds mission, or my area of expertise, I found myself taking on some of these cases. Since we did not have a shelter or a developed adoption program, these tasks were very time-consuming and draining. Trying to meet the needs of these animals and people deserving of help, but in situations that were not part of our mission, took time and energy away from the specific areas of concern that had necessitated the creation of Blessed Bonds in the first place. While it often felt emotionally painful not to be able to help in some of these instances, we quickly learned to build our referral base and direct people in need to other organizations who specialized in helping people and animals in those particular situations. Although we wanted to help in multiple ways, we chose to focus on helping in the ways that our small group was designed and best equipped to handle. For example, we fostered a senior poodle while her owner was in the hospital, and referred a person who wanted to find a new family for two dogs with special needs to an organization with a well-established adoption program in place.

SET LIMITS ANYWAY!

Go against your natural desire to give without setting limits. If you are truly in it for the long haul—and believe that you will always strive to help animals attain better lives—sustain that passion by placing it into a life that balances your personal needs with the altruistic desires of your heart. If you left it up to your feelings, you would rarely say no and that will not work. SET THOSE LIMITS! While there are always exceptions to every rule, in general, in order to succeed in setting limits you need to have guidelines set up for you and your group *before* you find yourself or your group in over your head. Some examples of limit-setting that successful groups have employed include putting time between a request and a return call or email rather than an immediate response, or keeping firm limits on the number of dogs and cats that are under an organization's care at one time. We already know that at this point in time none of us can do everything that we want to do, and while there will be times when we stretch our capacity, we need to consciously implement limits. We can only do so much. If we choose to ignore the need for limit setting and push beyond what we truly can handle, eventually the consequences will be ineffectiveness and an inability to help at all. Individuals get sick, burn out, and suffer from compassion fatigue, causing them to leave the field or not be able to help any animals at all for an indefinite amount of time. Organizations that become overfull often shut down. So limiting is inevitable, and it works better when we do it consciously and ahead of time. We can best decide the ways in which setting limits works for us so that we, as individuals and as groups, can truly continue to help in the long run.

A few years ago, my friend Tammy founded an organization that has made amazing progress in managing feral cats in the western suburbs of Chicago. When I asked her how she was able to get so many people to help she shared her secret and told me that she makes requests of others with careful deliberation. She purposely only asks each person to help in a way that she believes is aligned with that individual's strengths, and well within the limits of his or her current situation. She works very hard to not use guilt tactics or cause undue stress in a person's life, by her request. While some of her core volunteers do a lot, she also has a lot of people doing just a little; that is, enough to still contribute to her work, but not cause stress in their lives.

Tammy also shared with me a personal example of her own limit setting. Since her organization's inception, she has fostered cats in the basement of the house that she shares with her longtime partner. She told me that while he has always supported her efforts, he also had expressed a personal desire to decrease the number of cats they housed. Last year, when their basement was flooded, Tammy's partner helped transport the foster cats to safety with a sore back and without a complaint. Tammy said that it was at that moment she decided that she could honor his request for fewer cats in the house by taking this opportunity to no longer foster cats in the basement. The end result was that she now had more time to use her talents of leadership and ingenuity to help move the organization forward, while her partner was given more time and space to do some of the other things that he wanted to do. Both were happier. And it may surprise you to know that although she stopped personally fostering cats the number of cats her organization took into foster care actually increased. Because she reduced her time caring for foster cats, she was able to put more effort into an activity that accentuated her exceptional natural ability to get more people to help.

PACE YOURSELF

Slow down. Remember that loving animals is twenty-four hours a day, seven days a week. It does not leave you because it *is* you. It is a lifestyle, a passion, a way of life, a philosophy of living. Some people have jobs that they intensely attend to for eight hours a day, then they leave their work at the office. Animal advocates, on the other hand, are aware of animals that may be in need all of the time and anytime of the day or night. By nature, the advocate's heart is also attuned to stories that might suggest an animal in need. For example, an animal advocate becomes concerned for the feral cats that may inhabit the island in which they were vacationing. Friends and relatives know whom to contact when an animal question or situation arises. An advocate feels compelled to help the stray on the street, or the neighbor asking for advice on training. Most animal advocates have either foster pets or their own furry family at home, and are in contact with veterinarians, pet walkers, pet groomers, and animal welfare organizations as they simply go about their everyday lives. Hearing about an animal in need is a common occurrence. Those who are vegetarians and vegans are aware of issues surrounding the plight of animals every time they eat or are with others who are eating. Advocates of wildlife notice the squirrel without the tail or the neighbor's window that the birds continue to fly into and feel compelled to take action. Loving animals is a twenty-four seven proposition. Since there are no natural breaks, it is up to you to set the limits and live by them, so you can continue to be at your best for the animals.

OVER THE LIMIT

Although it cost me a day's time and $450.00, I still consider one particular speeding ticket to be a bargain. I received it a few years ago, and it gave me a valuable lesson about staying within reasonable limits—a lesson that goes way beyond simply staying within speed limits while driving. I was coming back from having brought two cats to a foster home about an hour away. The traffic was terrible and the trip took an extra forty-five minutes. Driving back toward home, I was hungry and in a hurry, hoping to make it to the vet to pick up prescription dog food for another foster before the vet office closed at eight o'clock that evening. When the traffic lessened and the road was clear I sped down it, going forty-seven miles an hour in a thirty-five mile an hour zone, which then changed to twenty miles an hour near a church—a traffic violation serious enough to necessitate a court date.

I was to appear at one o'clock on a Wednesday afternoon. Ironically, it was scheduled on a day that I had a commitment to give a talk on self-care of the giving heart. The policeman informed me that this was not an acceptable reason to miss court. I would need to hire someone to appear in my place or change this prior commitment.

I took my inconvenient and costly speeding ticket to heart and decided I would never get another one and I would slow down my life. The first step I took to prove to myself that I meant business was to reschedule my Wednesday morning clients so I would not be rushing to court from work in the afternoon. I had a relaxing morning with the dogs and drove slowly down to the courthouse, arriving over an hour early. I allowed extra time in case I got lost, and certainly did not want to take a chance of getting a speeding ticket on my way there. With over an hour to spare, I found a cute little café that offered a lunch option that happened to be one of my favorite comfort foods: a baked potato with a side order of broccoli covered with honey mustard dressing and a cup of coffee. I sat down at a table and began writing the following lesson to myself:

> *I am taking my gift of a speeding ticket to heart. I am enjoying my lunch and I am not taking out all kinds of paperwork that I had brought along in a bag in case there was extra time. Rather, I am relaxing and listening to some songs from the 70s that are playing in a jukebox of this cafe and reminiscing about who I was and what I was doing when I was a teenager at the time those songs were popular.*

In contemplating my lesson, I also recalled how it did not seem to matter in the least bit to the officer assigning me the ticket that I had saved the lives of two cats. He didn't praise me for my good deed; I had broken a safety law and was going to pay the price, of which totaled $450, between fines and a lawyer's fee. But I embraced the gift of the speeding ticket that day and made a personal commitment to slow down. The court ruled that the ticket would not go on my record as long as I did not accrue another ticket of a similar kind for the next six months. With that added incentive, along with my own realization that I must slow down for my own wellbeing as well as that of others, I began to move physically and mentally at a slower, more comfortable pace. I continue to this day to approach each day this same way. I so much more enjoy driving within the speed limit wherever I go, even when other drivers are risking head-on collisions to pass me. I have further incorporated this lesson into my life to include the pace at which I generally walk and move about. I no longer find myself tripping over the dogs or bumping into my husband as I rush around the house trying to quickly fit one more task into my day. I do not rush to the phone if it is in the other room, even when I may not be able to pick it up before it goes to voicemail. I even limit the number of thoughts I allow myself to think to just one at a time—and sometimes with space in between! Slowing down is a much more pleasant existence for me and I am sure it must be more enjoyable for those who are around me. I highly recommend it!

While setting limits can initially feel like you are letting down the animals, once you put this practice in action you will discover that you not only have more peace and enjoyment in your life, but you are enhancing your ability to help more animals.

CHAPTER VI
BALANCING STRATEGY: LETTING GO

LETTING GO

"Letting go" means removing the thoughts we have that give us a sense of false control over our journey, over the journeys of others, and even over the journeys of animals. The false belief that we are in charge results in guilt, worry, and disappointment in ourselves, and in others, when life does not work out as we had planned. Rather than releasing our grip on what we cannot control, we push even harder because we believe that letting go means letting down the animals. In reality, however, when we let go of this false sense of control, clarity and creativity have a chance to flow freely and help us meet challenges. We become more effective in making that difference in the lives of animals.

TAKE IT FROM FAITH

You can only move forward when you let go of the past, let go of attachments, and let go of self-importance. I started Dogtown at Best Friends. I had a hand in every aspect of it right from the start—how the dogs were housed, fed, cared for, and who got to come there. I lived and breathed Dogtown. I spent hours every day watching dogs interact with each other. I reveled in the dynamics of their relationships and how they communicated with each other. It was a wonderful time.

As Dogtown grew, I realized it needed more than I could give. I am not a natural manager. It's a skill I admire, but knew I was not that person to help guide Dogtown past a certain level of operation. For example, it felt important to me that I would always remember each and every dog. But as hundreds of dogs passed in front of my eyes, it became harder to hold them all in my head. This was no longer the right sized operation for me. Time to let go.

Letting go meant handing over the reins of the daily routines to others who could create the sustainable structure needed to take Dogtown into the future. Letting go means allowing others to grow and flourish. It means allowing the introduction of new ideas and new ways of helping the animals move on to new homes. As a result, this will save more and more animals.

I have observed over the last thirty-plus years how hard this stage is for many people. Letting go means losing control over the outcome. And that is the point. When we try to control every aspect of life we have to keep everything relatively small and manageable and that may work against our broader goals. "There is nothing like a diagnosis of a life threatening heart disease to focus your attention," said Marilou Chanrasmi, president of MnPAW, an animal welfare coalition for Minnesota, and co-founder of Leech Lake Legacy, created to assist animals in need from the Leech Lake Indian Reservation in Minnesota. Marilou has a rare, unpredictable, and untreatable heart condition. At any moment, her heart's ability to function could significantly change or she could continue along as she is for an indefinite amount of time. Marilou feels a sense of urgency in using the gifts that she has to help animals as much as possible while she still can. She describes this diagnosis as a gift in that it has helped her to see what really matters. When she sees herself or others doing things that take time away from the animals she has learned to reframe those emotions rather than become consumed in petty arguments. "I appreciate every moment I am given, and want to make the most of every day," she explains. Because Marilou has learned to let go of the anxiety, anger, and worry that comes with a life-threatening illness, she has found herself able to let go of her "need to control everything" and this "frees up so much energy to do the lifesaving work we want to do for the animals." Marilou attributes this simple act of letting go as the dominant factor in the formation and growth of two successful rescue organizations that have saved hundreds of lives of animals in less than two years.

LETTING GO OF YOUR JOURNEY

Again, to begin within, let's start with your sense of control over your own journey with the animals. Many advocates feel haunted by the daily thoughts that they are not doing enough to help animals. Do you find yourself asking the question, "What is taking me so long to get this organization off the ground and making more of a difference?" Perhaps you feel guilt and regret about those things you have not yet done, or resentment toward whomever or whatever you feel may have gotten in your way of doing more. Can you consider accepting the way life is right now and embracing the belief that you are where you need to be?

TIMING

Understanding and accepting that life happens in its own time is essential to learning to let go. Just because we want something to happen now does not mean that it is the best time for it to take place. For example, perhaps society is not yet ready to support a particular new idea that you have, but it will be embraced later in its own time. Or maybe it is during those extra years that you spend working at the non-animal related job you were hoping to quit that you meet the other like-minded people who will help you attain your goal at a later time. It may be that what feels like an obstacle to your dream is really a necessary step to the place you are meant to go. Your love and compassion for animals matters, even when you cannot see its direct impact. Learn to let go of your time frame and allow life to happen according to its own.

"Standing on the shoulder of giants" is a familiar phrase used to reflect the idea that sometimes it isn't really the one person or one organization that attains a goal single-handedly, even when it appears so; it is the work of many who came before that made the whole thing possible. Applied to the animal welfare world, it reminds us that every act of kindness toward animals, no matter how big or small, contributes to the positive energy that is going toward them. No longer feeling pressured to hurry up and help, we can be reassured that simply being our best in the moment at hand contributes to the shared movement toward a better world for all living beings.

BE WHERE YOU ARE

These four simple words make up the answer to

the question that I am often asked by frustrated animal advocates: How do I know I am on the right path? One of the obstacles that block the everyday joy in the animal lover's life is the persistent thought that they are not where they should be in the world of helping animals. They admire the animal welfare pioneers and feel like they are not doing enough and, again, they believe they are letting them down. They believe that things keep happening that get in the way of them being able to be where they want to be. What would it be like to accept a new thought that the journey you are on right now is exactly where you need to be?

PERSONAL STORY

I experienced frustration in what I perceived to be a holdup in arriving on my purposeful path to help animals. I believed that many unexpected life events continued to get in the way. Now, looking back, I can clearly see that each and every experience that I labeled a delay was vital to the path I am presently on; I am where I need to be now, and always have been where I needed to be on that path. The perceived obstacles all played a part in helping me to recognize and develop the best ways for me to help animals.

My husband's and my dream of having enough capital to start an animal sanctuary in 2001 plummeted along with our financial investments in the stock market. I was faced with the disappointment of what seemed like just another in a long line of roadblocks standing in the way of one of my most important goals in life: starting an animal sanctuary. I can see now that I was only being re-routed on my unique path that would honor my passion to help animals while keeping me aligned with the best way I could use my gifts. So rather than retiring and starting a sanctuary as I had hoped, I began to explore other ways to help animals. I started and ran a foster-based nonprofit organization and continued to work as a clinical psychologist. It became clear to me that although my dream was to start a sanctuary it would not have been the best choice for me. The decline in the value of our financial investments was not a barrier; it caused a change in plans that helped me find the path that allows me to give in a way that is most aligned with who I am.

But I didn't come to those insights easily or quickly. I lived with a nagging thought that I was not doing enough for the animals; I was not getting there fast enough. At times, I have even viewed my decision to become a psychologist as interfering with attaining my heart's true desires. This misleading thought blocked me from experiencing the full joy that I now feel in my clinical work with people. Furthermore, I see that my psychological training and experience were necessary prerequisites for creating and developing an organization dedicated to preserving the valuable bond between people and pets.

Everything unfolded when I stopped trying to knock down the perceived barriers and stopped believing that life was getting in the way. When my beloved dog Blackie developed lymphoma his treatment and care became a top priority, and without hesitation I was able to put my dreams of starting any kind of animal welfare organization on hold—I let go. Ironically, it was by letting go and embracing my journey with Blackie that the first step toward the creation of Blessed Bonds would happen while he was undergoing treatment. The nature of my dog's illness and treatment necessitated that we spend many hours per week at my vet clinic, resulting in forming closer relationships between me and Blackie's veterinarians and other staff. It was during one of Blackie's chemotherapy treatments that a vet technician and I discussed the workings of an organization that would help people and pets stay together by providing temporary foster care for their pets. One veterinarian joined in on the discussion and offered to help with the veterinary care that would be part of such a program. The other veterinarian became a founding board member for Blessed Bonds. The inception of Blessed Bonds emerged as I let go of my plans to start a sanctuary and the forced timeline in my head, and honored my natural desire to provide Blackie with the most compassionate care possible during his illness. All the time I spent with Blackie's vet staff to treat his condition did not delay my dream to help animals, but actually became the impetus to the formation of Blessed Bonds.

Let Go and Then What?

So now that you are primed to let go, perhaps you are asking what part of your journey *is* in your control. It is in your control to accept what is. Accept who you are, be where you are, and be the best that you can be in any given moment in time and at any given place that you find yourself on your path. That's all. You can refrain from judging life events as obstacles and failures, and be open to whatever unfolds as all part of your journey. Every moment leading up to now brings you to where you are. All of the worries and fears that you conjure up in your mind will not stop your path from taking you where it wants you to go. Letting go of those depleting thoughts will allow you to fully embrace the joy and the gifts in the surprises and the mystery in the unknowing. Can you take the pressure off by allowing yourself only to be fully where you are today—right now?

Letting Go of a Role

Sometimes the worry about letting down the animals can result in an animal advocate staying with a helping role that may not be the best fit. This need to let go of our position may present itself in the form of feeling "stuck." The inability to let go is often accompanied by feelings of helplessness and despair. In addition to feeling drained of energy, depleted of joy, and without peace of mind, there is a sense of hopelessness, a belief that there is no way out that is causing the distress. There is no emotional relief in sight. While still dedicated to helping animals, individuals feeling this way may have lost the joy in their lives. They are not able to find their way out of the exhaustion and depletion. Many animal advocates report feeling stuck and have told me that they feel like the only way out of their present discomfort is to die. While some have expressed thoughts of suicide, most of these individuals explain that they are worn out, but that they plan to continue to persevere. They consider living with despair as part of the necessary sacrifice to help the animals. Animal advocates who reach this place are often being challenged to let go in a deeper way than they had ever considered. They may need to let go of their current role in animal welfare—perhaps a role that now feels like an ingrained part of their identity. It is easy to become attached to the way that you have found to help animals and hard to give it up, even when it may be necessary for your own wellbeing.

How does this happen? You enthusiastically begin to help animals. Perhaps you answer the phone calls for your organization, assist in the medical care of abused animals, foster behaviorally challenged dogs, or select the dogs and cats at the local pound that your group will be most able to help. You may have fallen into a particular pattern of helping that you feel compelled to continue.

This work may be depleting you and may not be the best use of your gifts, but you believe that others expect you to help in that way. You may feel that the animals are counting on you. So you have tried to find a way to continue with joy, but you are in distress. You have already tried taking a new perspective. You realize that it does not matter if you take more breaks, nurture yourself, or have even found others to assist you; this way that you have been helping animals is no longer working for you. Yet, it feels like abandonment to give it up. You cannot let down the animals that you believe have counted on you to be there. Your heart knows that you are in need of a *game changer*; that is, you need to let go of the role that is draining you so you can help animals from a place of peace and joy. Give yourself permission to take the leap out of where you are and into somewhere new. It is important to remember that there are people who love animals with all kinds of passion and talents. Perhaps somebody with a natural inclination to the work that you were doing can take over your role.

EXAMPLE

A good friend of mine started a successful rescue group overseas. His day-to-day work involved working with animals in desperate need of help. He struggled with depression, burnout, exhaustion, and an inability to find joy in his life. He viewed his emotional pain as a weakness in character and felt he would be letting down the animals if he left his position. He saw no alternative other than to sacrifice his own physical, mental, and emotional wellbeing. Family circumstances transplanted him back to the United States and he was forced to let go of the role he had carved out for himself, and change the way that he used his gifts to help animals. After years of struggling with guilt and anxiety regarding his desire to get out, physical distance necessitated that he give up his role as leader and crisis manager working directly with the rescue of animals. He now realizes that his authentic way to help animals and maintain his own sanity is to help without direct contact with the animals in need of help. My friend is now able to enjoy his life in new ways without carrying the burden of the pain that stayed with him when working directly with the animals in need. He still works closely, but remotely, to support the organization that he founded overseas; others are able to do the hands-on work that he once did. He now experiences joy in his everyday life and joy in what he does for the animals. He finds that he can meet the challenges with a clear and calm state of mind and knows he is making a difference in the lives of the animals by helping in ways that come easily and naturally to him. As my friend discovered, sometimes it takes strength to recognize when your way of helping has become depleting and find a way to continue to help that is more aligned with who you are and what you can do.

Letting Go of Emotional Pain

Feeling "stuck" can also be an indication of a hurt in your heart that needs to be released and healed. Perhaps you need to let go of an emotional pain that has crept into your everyday life and is blocking your ability to find joy. I have seen this resistance to happiness, and the need for healing a lingering hurt, present itself in the monthly pet loss support group that I facilitate. People sometimes become trapped by painful memories of their beloved pets' death. This emotional pain may express itself with haunting images, repetitive thoughts racing through their minds, and the inability to find peace within themselves. Until they can recognize and release the pain or self-blaming perceptions around the event, the hurt may continue to overwhelm them. Getting the help one needs to let go of the pain is the first step to getting unstuck and allowing one's best and most joyful self to emerge once again.

LETTING GO OF THE JOURNEYS OF OTHERS

Animal advocates' desires to change others is usually well intended; they believe that getting others to change will be better for the animals. While it is normal to want others to change in accordance with how we see things and what we believe is best for everyone, it is not within our ability to change others. We need to let go of our efforts to direct others' thoughts and behaviors. We do not have that power. What we can do is accept people exactly where they are on their life's journey; that is, where they will be whether we choose to accept it or not. What to us might seem like such an easy and necessary change for someone to make, may not be for that person. When we are able to look back on our own life's journey and accept the places we have been it sometimes is easier to understand and accept where someone else might currently be. Case in point: Although I have not eaten meat in almost thirty years, or dairy products for seventeen years, there was a time when I did, and I still loved and cared deeply for animals. It is important for me and other vegans to remember our own personal histories when we see our animal-loving friends eating meat or dairy foods. It is important to remember that we, too, were once not ready to change our diets, even though we may have continued to care for animals in other ways. And we can still continue to show others all that veganism offers with the knowledge that role modeling is one of the most effective methods for change in others.

I am able to see how my acquisition of knowledge and experiences throughout the years has sharpened my sensitivity to the plight of animals and how I've made changes in my daily life accordingly so as to not support animal suffering. But I can also look back on my journey and see many times when I made decisions that did not always work out in the best way for the animals. For example, I remember re-homing a cat without realizing that she could easily escape the new home and get lost; she did escape and did get lost. With the experience and knowledge I have acquired now, it is standard practice for me to discuss with a new adopting family the challenges of keeping their new cat healthy and safe indoors. I like to think that my words increase the chances of the cat not becoming lost from his or her new home, but at the same time, I realize that I cannot control everything I would like to so I do my best and let go. I also forgive myself for the mistakes I have made in the past when adopting out an animal, and I forgive others who have done the same. A humane educator told me about a workshop that she attended where the participants engaged in an exercise in which they were given information about potential adopters, and then asked to make a decision as to whether to let that person adopt a pet. In this exercise, all the potential adopters were denied a pet based on something that they described on the mock application. Then it was revealed that the applicants were all the participants in their group. The point of the exercise was to recognize that we all have been at different places on our journeys; we need to accept where we are and where others are, too—without judgment. We cannot put ourselves in control of the progression of their personal growth and development.

So what does letting go of the journeys of others look like? We still may express our own genuine views and opinions, but we need to also let go of what others do with that information. Their decisions can only be up to them. In other words, make your own decision as to whether you need to say something, and go ahead and follow through with compassion and understanding. Then, let it go. Accept that any changes that occur in another person must come from within that person. It may help in our quest to let go of changing others to realize that there are those out there who want to change us! For example, my niece has pointed out to me the ways that I could become more conscientious in my recycling. She was surprised to discover some habits that she expected me not to have as an environmentally responsible person. Although I certainly care about the environment, having been so consumed with my own passions, I have not taken the time to change every bad habit when it comes to the environment, something that my niece feels it would be so easy to do. I can only imagine the many other ways I may be offending someone by the way I live, an advocate whose passion and expertise in some particular area that is beyond my present understanding.

Of course, we want to change the people who seem insensitive to the wellbeing of animals. These groups might include the general public, as well as our neighbors, friends, family, and acquaintances, people giving up their animals, and animal advocates who we feel are not totally aligned with our values in how they relate to animal welfare. I am sure you have encountered people who seem to get in the way of what you are trying to do to make a difference in the lives of the deserving animals.

Sometimes the people we really want to change the most are those fellow animal advocates working beside us. We expect them to be on our side, to take the actions we believe are needed to help the animal best. We expect them to see things the way we do. We expect them to change when given the right information. Time and time again I have been asked to help mediate disagreements over minor philosophical differences between and within groups of animal advocates that cause major schisms and upheaval. Individuals become angry and separate themselves from others who were once their allies. How many animal rescue organizations were formed as a result of internal wars and an inability to accept the different views of another? How many have folded altogether because of an inability of the members to accept each other?

We must let go of changing people and learn to work together with them if we are ever to make the kind of vast strides we want to make in animal welfare. Of course, when given the opportunity you can share your wisdom with others. You can model effective communication, mentor if asked, and suggest strategies for compromise and team building. Sometimes working together means choosing to work peacefully alongside a group that helps animals even though they may have views quite different than your group. It always concerns me when I hear someone say that they are helping animals because they "love animals, but hate people." This formula simply does not work, as the animals are counting on us to find them families and work together to give them better lives. Helping animals requires people to work in harmony, and letting go of the need to change others is an essential part of that cooperative spirit.

LETTING GO OF THE JOURNEY OF ANIMALS

While we all want the animals that we have helped to go on and lead their own lives without us, it is not always easy to accept that our role in their journey has ended and we need to let go of them. Our lives intersected; we played a part in their journey and now we need to let go of it. We may need to let others help or share in their lives and allow the animals to make new relationships. Perhaps we were instrumental in finding a homeless pet a new family, but now it's time to trust that they can take it from here and do not need us anymore. They need the chance to use their charm and endear themselves to the new family as they did to you. It is important to remember that they have their own life journey to fulfill, too. They need to be able to continue on their way without you, and lead their own lives in the new circumstances you have helped find for them. They need to fulfill their unique purpose.

LETTING GO OF THE WHAT IFS

Sometimes it is the "what ifs" we tell ourselves that keeps us from fully letting go of the animal's journey. This expression is commonly heard at pet loss support group meetings when grieving people struggle to come to terms with the decisions that they made when their pets were at the end of their lives. They wonder what would have happened if they would have seen the signs of illness earlier, or if they would have chosen not to do the surgery—or not euthanize the pet at that time. Second-guessing is common: Should we have gone to a different veterinarian? Those who have chosen new adoptive families for the pets in their care often find themselves asking the "what if" question when things do not work out as expected. What if we would have adopted the dog to a different family? the animal rescue worker may wonder. What if this or what if that? It's endless. If we want our giving ability to endure, we need to counter the "what ifs' with our own understanding that we do the best we can with what we know at the time. We act out of love for those in our care, and that is all we can ever expect ourselves to do. The reality is that we can never know what the other roads would have looked like had the animal's journey taken a different path.

Personal Story

I remember a cat that came through the Blessed Bonds program when his human companion became ill. We nicknamed him Houdini because he would go to great lengths to try to escape his confinement indoors. We assumed that having lived outdoors for his first six months of life might have contributed to his resistance to being a strictly indoor cat. When his owner passed away our organization went through great lengths to ensure a new adoptive home that would be able to keep him safely inside. In addition to being a wonderful loving home, the family lived in a condominium on the third floor with doors to the outside on every floor. Six doors would all need to be left open at once for him to escape. After a wonderful year in his new home, the family moved to California to live with relatives and Houdini finally got his chance to escape and took it. When a family member with declining mental functioning inadvertently left a door open in the middle of the night, Houdini left. So many precautions were taken, but this accident still occurred. Houdini never returned, and although we were all saddened by his leaving we can only wonder if perhaps finding a way to live outside again was an inevitable part of his journey.

Letting Go of Self-Importance

It is easy to unknowingly fall into the "only me" way of thinking, or, in other words, to believe that an animal will only be okay if you personally are the one to help. While we may think we are only acting responsibly and in the best interest of the animals, our actions sometimes are really saying any of the following:

I am the only one who can do right by this pet.

I am the best home.

I am the one with whom this dog or cat is most bonded. This animal adores me and wants to live with me.

Our rescue group is the only one that can do right by this animal.

In the following section, Faith relates the time early in her rescue days when she realized she had been living under the assumption that some dogs must only have her, and the relief it brought her to let go of this idea.

TAKE IT FROM FAITH

In the early days of Best Friends, I was the unofficial animal control and would respond to calls from local law enforcement for a variety of dog issues, from stray dogs hanging around a neighborhood to vicious bites. I would load said dog in the front of my small Nissan truck and off we would go for the five miles from town to the sanctuary.

I began to notice that in all cases during that short journey each dog would start to focus very intently on me.

It was a small cab, but despite what had happened prior to this unexpected trip—for the dog that is—the dog was doing his or her best to work his or her magic on me. The dog had just been wrenched from their home in the case of a bite incident, or been wandering around lost looking for food or a place to stay, but now their eyes and body were targeting me as the next provider.

"You're just a floozy," I said to one dog that was cozying up to me like I was a long lost relative. But it made sense. It was an "Aha!" for me. Dogs are hardwired to look for both companionship and for resources. One's gone (previous home or circumstances), now it's time for another one and you will do very nicely.

Instead of feeling disappointed that the myth of a dog's loyalty to its master was discredited, I was elated. This meant that if a dog wanted to be my best friend in five short miles of roadway then he or she would bond to a new adopter quickly and easily. In a way, it was profoundly liberating. It's easy to fall into the trap of being special to an animal. That's not to say we aren't, but we are all a bit interchangeable as far as they are concerned. Understanding our furry friends can make it easier for us to let go of the animals into another family's loving care.

Life Goes On

The reality is that life can and does go on without any one of us. None of us are indispensible. Sure, events will unfold differently without our presence and influence; the animals whose lives we would have touched will take different paths, but these will still be their own journeys. This point became real to me when I came close to being hit by a truck on a very busy street right outside my office. As I was getting out of the driver's side of my car, I saw a pickup truck with a young driver and another young man in the front seat coming toward me. I do not know if they were purposely trying to scare me or just playing with me, but I noticed the smiles on their faces as their car suddenly veered full speed ahead toward me as if it was meant to hit me as I stepped out of my car into the street. I quickly backed my body up against my car and cringed, hoping I was out of their way but also wondering if I was about to be hit. I remember expecting to feel the sensation of the front end of their car against my body. It seemed to me that their truck missed me by less than an inch, and I was relieved to realize that I was still standing, unhurt. I remember thinking moments later how close I came to finding myself with broken bones in a hospital bed or possibly even having been killed. This incident caused a moment of vivid realization about something I'd faintly known all along. If something had happened to me, the people and animals in my life would continue on with their journeys. Their paths would change in some ways without my influencing their lives at that moment in time, but their journeys would go on. Similarly, dogs and cats and people all over the world were living their lives without me. While I knew my efforts were still valuable, I also became more acutely aware of the fact that there are other people helping animals, there are going to be people helping animals when I am gone, as there were people helping animals before I did. Each one of us matters, but we are still only one of many.

Personal Story

Two of my own cats, Jade and Maverick, taught me about letting go of self-importance and allowing them to have their own journeys. Jade was left in a box down the street from an animal shelter in which I volunteered, along with her three newborn kittens. Maverick, a big orange tabby, was one of her kittens that was adopted by my brother-in-law Anthony. Jade became part of our family, and five years later, Maverick came to live with us when my brother-in-law passed away. I knew that it was unlikely that the cats remembered that they were mother and son, but nonetheless Jade adored Maverick and snuggled up with him every chance she could for the next twelve years. Jade developed cancer and was not able to recover from her last surgery. She spent her remaining three days of life with her favorite living being in the whole world at her side: Maverick. I saw that he was taking wonderful care of her and she was where she wanted to be. While there are times when admitting a pet to the vet hospital or deciding on euthanasia to relieve suffering at the end of life may be the compassionate choice, I believe that each situation requires its own heartfelt evaluation as to how to best proceed. In this case, I believed that Jade was getting what she needed at home with Maverick. I moved a litter box, food, and water close to the two cats so Maverick could choose to be continually at her side; and that is what he did. The hour that she passed away, I had my arms wrapped around both of them; Maverick had his mother wrapped in a full body hug, purring loudly and continuously until she peacefully passed away. He remained in her bed with her for an additional two hours before coming up to me and burying his head in my lap when he was ready to receive his own comfort from me. Maverick and Jade taught me a valuable lesson in the importance of letting go of control of the animals' journeys.

We are each on a path and each animal is on his or hers. Our journeys may intersect for a moment, a few days, or a lifetime. So many factors converge that determine which roads cross. When we let go of the need to control our own journey, and that of others and of the animals, we take a big step in being our best. Not only do we find more joy and peace in our own lives, but we pass it on to the people and animals whom our lives intersect.

CHAPTER VII
BALANCING STRATEGY: LISTEN

LISTEN TO THE HEART

Balancing your innermost needs with your desires to help others requires full attention to the voice of your heart, especially during the more challenging times, such as after the loss of an animal friend. With the exception of some birds and turtles, the animals that you give to, live with, and act as an advocate for will probably have a shorter lifespan than you. Saying goodbye is an inevitable part of this journey of the soul led by your heart's desire to give to animals. Since you will connect with many animals, some directly under your care and others that evoke your concern from a distance, you are likely to experience sadness and grief multiple times in your life. Listening to the wisdom of your loving heart can help you continue to feel the peace and joy that is still there even through these challenging times.

TAKE IT FROM FAITH

When Prince Charming died, I was devastated. The seven-year-old, six-pound black Chihuahua had stolen my heart and he was gone from my life way too soon. Liver cancer had invaded his body and he succumbed to it. I had adopted him from the Arizona Humane Society when his person could no longer care for him. He was especially close to my heart because he was by my side when the idea of starting a no-kill sanctuary was just being tossed around by those of us who would soon start Best Friends Animal Sanctuary.

I took his death hard. Loss is something all of us animal people live with all the time and I have experienced it many times since Prince passed on. For Carla Phillips, a dog hospice foster mom working in partnership with Best Friends Animal Society and other rescue programs, loss is something she has come to accept as part of her life. Since 2007 Carla has opened her home and her heart to forty-eight terminally ill dogs; thirty-eight of them have passed on. Carla is often asked how she copes with experiencing loss so frequently. "It isn't about me; it's about the dogs," Carla will tell them. "I can feel sad as each dog passes, but then I need to be open to receive another dog who deserves a home for his or her final days, and there are a lot of them."

Carla's home is decked out with a lot of comfortable beds and blankets. Water bowls are everywhere and feeding the nine or ten residents is often a lengthy undertaking, as most of the dogs require special medicine or treatments. Carla makes sure that dogs of all ages and sizes spend whatever time they may have left in a warm, welcoming environment. They listen to the TV and hear the click of knitting needles, along with all of the other normal sounds of a home: the doorbell, the dishwasher, the vacuum, and the hum of the fridge. The varied length of time that the dogs spend with her illustrates her ability to live with uncertainty. The following statement shows her commitment to honoring the unique needs of each dog as they live out their final days in her loving home: "Negrita was in the first group of dogs I brought to my house. The staff at the sanctuary felt she would not last a week she was so ill, but she lived with me for three weeks—three weeks knowing she was in a home." Carla fondly reminisced about Buddy, the poodle mix who lived with her for two years and three months, and Bailey, a black pug with multiple medical problems who stayed with her for fourteen months. Carla reminisces about other dogs that came to stay with her:

> [I remember] Rusty the Chow Chow who was only here for about five months. Prince, on the other hand, was a very large but almost feral dog who stayed with me a bit over two years. Zuma, the most emotionally scarred, was here for about two months. She had been chained every day of her life in the direct Arizona sun with no shade. Magic Man was with me for about eighteen months. His loss was especially hard because I really was not prepared; I had hoped to have him a long time.

Each one of the thirty-eight dogs who have passed through her life at the point of me writing this is buried and remembered at Angels Rest, the memorial park at Best Friends Animal Sanctuary. Carla's gift to every dog that has passed through her life is an engraved marker stone. Each dog has his or her own placement ceremony where a small group of friends will gather to support Carla and tell stories about their experiences with the dog, share a laugh, cry, and say a final goodbye as that dog is placed in the ground with loving care. A basket of polished stones is offered to all in attendance so they may choose a stone that speaks to them and place it on the site. This is a tradition in many religions and cultures around the world, and is a way of connecting to the memory of the person—or, in this case, the animal—buried there.

The Blessing is a ceremony held on the last Thursday of every month at Angels Rest at Best Friends Animal Sanctuary to honor the animals that have died that month. Come rain or shine, we gather together to share stories about the lives of those who are not with us anymore. It's sad at times, funny at other times, but always significant to take the time to remember what those precious lives have meant to us.

Some form of ritual can play a role in the healing of loss. It can be re-living a memory in a group, like the one at The Blessing, or on your own with a poem, a painting, a photo montage, or putting a favorite toy out on the bookshelf. Individuals need to find their own way of remembering and honoring their beloved furry friends when they have passed away.

Unblocking the Voice of Your Own Heart

Because "blessed bonds" so wonderfully describes the relationships we have with animals—that is, divine connections full of immeasurable blessings—I chose that name for the charitable organization that I founded in 2004. Blessed Bonds is dedicated to preserving and promoting the human-animal companion bond. Among the multiple gifts that our blessed bonds with animals give to us are unconditional love, faithful companionship, and a daily reliable constant in our lives. These incredible connections bring purpose, meaning, laughter, and soulfulness to everyday life. And we love how we are when we are with the animals! They bring out the best in us, keep us in the present moment, and model for us how to take care of ourselves. Listening to the heart can get us through the sadness and distress we naturally feel when our animal friends leave this Earth. Having facilitated a pet loss support group for many years, I have noticed, however, that there are three common beliefs that arise in times of loss that keep us from accessing the heart's wisdom. These self-depleting thoughts block the peacefulness and bury the joy that is innate to the journey. Grieving animal lovers often draw the following three conclusions that keep them from hearing the comfort that their compassionate hearts have to offer during these challenging times:

1. *I feel guilty.*

2. *I can't go on.*

3. *I am afraid I will forget.*

Recognizing the flaws in these thoughts and viewing them as obstacles can help us uncover the wisdom of the heart, dismiss the thoughts, and restore the peace and joy that our lives with animals always continues to give us.

1. *I feel guilty.*

Guilt is a common emotion experienced at the time of loss. People find all kinds of reasons to take blame for what has happened. Owners often ask, "Why didn't I notice their illness sooner?" or say, "My pet was not ready to go and I hurried it." Owners often feel remorse and regret, feeling they might have made a wrong decision. A family may worry that the death was their fault because perhaps they gave their dog too many table scraps, or an owner might second guess the decision they made to forego a specific treatment or opting for surgery. The caregivers in animal shelters and those identified with being rescuers may blame themselves because a dog or cat in their care did not live out his or her life with a family asking, "Why didn't I try harder to find him a home?" or saying, "I should have done more." Guilt doesn't stop there. Some owners feel guilty because they are not feeling "as sad as they should," comparing their grief to somebody else's or even to previous losses they have had. We become trapped by thoughts that are not likely to be true, but that drag us down into a self-tormenting tragic view that blocks our hearts from celebrating an animal's life—no matter how long or short.

What do our compassionate hearts have to say about this guilt? The "what if" thoughts evoke guilty feelings even when we know in our hearts that we will never know what that "other path" would have been. Are any of these self-depleting guilty thoughts worth holding? Our inner wisdom tells us that all that any of us can ever do is make the best possible decision given everything in our life situation at that moment. What else can we possibly expect of ourselves? When we question our response to a loss our wise heart understands that each bond is unique with its own degree of sadness and accepts our variations in responses. When we listen to the heart, we remind ourselves that all of our actions came from love. We remember that our animal friends are on their own journey, too. We see the guilt for the obstacle that it is and let go of it.

2. *I can't go on.*

People report feeling devastated and heartbroken when they lose their beloved companions. Tears may fall from the smallest reminder. It is not uncommon for the yearning for the physical presence of one's dog or cat to become stronger through the first few months of adjusting to the loss. Sometimes the pain is described as greater than what pet owners experienced when beloved *human* friends and relatives had passed away, and the intensity of the pain leads them to believe they will not be able to bear it. Feeling deeply sad and empty are normal responses; "I can't go on," however, is a stressful thought that only blocks our access to the peace that is still available to us during these difficult times. This depleting belief can cause anxiety and even panic attacks because it takes us into the future where we are unable to imagine how we are going to adjust to the new world that will not have our loved one in it. It is common for grieving pet owners to say that just when they thought they were getting better in dealing with the loss, they were hit with a wave of unbearable sadness. They then question their ability to go on, and some people may even express a wish to die. When we let our hearts speak to us we realize that allowing ourselves to feel the sadness—as intense as it may be—is part of the strength that gets us through the loss. We only need to accept the feelings one day at a time, one moment at a time. When we stay in the present the fear of not being able to go on in the future dissipates and our hearts gently carry us through our grief.

The love created from the incredible bonds we shared continues to live on inside of us and offers the comfort that we need. What comforts you? Listening to the needs of the heart may lead individuals to a pet loss support group, a place where stories as well as coping strategies are shared among others in various stages of pet loss grief. Allow yourself to honor your unique needs; they are different for each of us. For example, some people may need to take off a day from work while others might prefer working extra hours. I knew a couple at the pet loss support group who chose to go away every weekend for the first two months after their beloved dog passed away. They both found it helpful to be away from all of the reminders of their usual weekend routine at home that they had with their furry family member. Some people find comfort in quiet music, favorite foods, reading, or going to bed early. Some owners report keeping their pets' food bowls and beds in the same place, while others prefer to remove all the visible reminders from their sight. There are those who have pictures all around their homes and say good morning and good night to the photographs every day. Others remove all pictures from view because they find them "too painful" to display. I could list many more of these differing coping strategies, but I think the point is clear: listen to what your heart needs without judgment. The fear-evoking thought that you will not be able to go on will find its way out of your mind.

3. *I am afraid I will forget.*

It is normal to want to keep all the animals we have had in our lives forever in our hearts. They have touched our soul, our very deepest core. They have changed us and left *paw prints* on our hearts forever. The thought, however, that we are afraid we will forget them can work against us and actually block our ability to remember the good times and feel their love in our hearts. The fear of forgetting them can cause us to hold onto the pain of the loss rather than accessing the love and joy that still remains within us. When we listen to the heart we can let go of these painful thoughts and realize every gift we have ever received from that bond. These treasured thoughts, feelings, traits, and mysteries continue to be part of us even after their physical presence is gone. So it is impossible for them to be forgotten. We are changed forever because of the bond we shared. The practice of listening to the heart allows us to continue to feel their spirits through that loving, soulful connection we had with them. One of our pet loss participants described the healing that had taken place for him over the year after he lost his best furry friend. He said that a hole was left in his heart when she passed away. The hole has not become smaller, but rather the love from that bond continues to grow in his heart, making his heart larger. He believes that in time he will share that growing capacity to love with a new animal companion. Another participant told the group that she had a breakthrough one night when she was dozing off to sleep and crying about her dog's death. She said that she suddenly felt a deep sense of gratitude for "getting to be the one" to share her life with her special companion for ten years. She realized that he was on his own journey, too, and remarked, "Of all the people in the world, how did I get to be so lucky?" While she still missed him terribly, she felt thankful for the privilege to have had this loving lifetime bond like no other.

In addition to the love we will always carry in our hearts, there are many ways to choose to honor and memorialize the animals that have left us. There are countless ways to ensure that we will not forget; we simply need to listen to the unique desires of each of our hearts. Personally, I find it comforting to write poems about the animals in my life after they have passed away. I do not seem to choose the time that I will write the tributes; when the time is right, the words will flow. I might add a favorite picture to the poem before sending it to friends and family. I have a friend who wears a locket that holds some of her cat's fur, another with a tattoo of her bunny on her arm. I have seen engraved garden stones, trees, and statues placed in memory of beloved pets. Some people have memorial services for their pets; others have special tributes to their pets set up in their homes. Some have pictures and ceramic paw prints while others prefer to keep nothing visible around them at all.

There is always joy in our journey with the animals. Every time we allow ourselves to find it, we are paying tribute to their lives. Many animal lovers feel that the greatest honor they can give to those pets that have passed away is to volunteer at shelters and give love to animals in need; some open their homes to foster dogs and cats. The memories of the times you spent together with your own pet, whether it was a comforting look, a soothing purr on your lap, a paw on your leg, or lick of a tear from your face, remind you that your beloved animal friend always had your best interest at heart. They still want you to be happy. They want you to celebrate life and live it to the fullest. I do not believe it is a stretch to assume that both parts of the bond—the human and the animal—want to know that although separated, each is happy. A phrase on a pet sympathy card from an unknown author reads, "Perhaps they are not the stars, but rather openings in

Heaven where the love of our lost ones pours through and shines down upon us to let us know they are happy."

So you can be assured that when you are ready to find love again and enjoy a new relationship with another furry companion, you are not betraying them, but only continuing their legacy of love and receiving their blessing. It does not take away from the love you shared with them; it honors that love. Lee Van Camp is an animal advocate who does hospice care for cats in her home. Her way of honoring those who have passed away is to continue to care for more cats in need of special care at the end of their lives. Even though the passing of each cat brings sadness to her heart, she focuses on the love that she is able to share and continue to give. She says, "Hundreds of cats are waiting for a home. It's true I get more attached to some than others and it's very sad when they pass, but I treat each cat as an individual and when it's their time, I am able to let go and embrace a new cat into my life."

Advocates may also find themselves distressed by the thought that they do not want to forget any animal across the world that has died tragically or too soon. These animals may include those who were prematurely euthanized or lived in abusive situations before they died, such as animals from factory and fur farms, research labs, neglectful families, and dog fighting rings. We do not need to keep replaying the haunting stories and painful images in our minds to remember even animals we've never met. We can choose to honor those who have died by continuing to work together to change the conditions for those animals that still have a chance at a better life going forward.

When we listen to the heart we realize that with the plight of animals in today's world it is not easy to embrace every day with peace and joy. We feel this challenge down to our very core. While we cannot remove the pain of animal loss from our hearts, we need to acknowledge it, and then focus on what uniquely brings us comfort. We may need to set limits on taking in the information that pains us and focus on what we are able to do every day. Many animal advocates have told me that while they first opened every email that described an animal in need, they have learned to limit the information they take in. We can choose to acknowledge the challenges while at the same time direct our focus constructively, in celebration of their lives and in appreciation of the fact that we get to share the planet with them. A friend of mine is a veterinarian who reviews videotapes of the mistreatment of factory farm animals. She explained to me that every night when cooking her vegan dinner she takes a few moments to light a candle, sit quietly, and say a little prayer in memory of the animals who may be suffering and for those who have passed away.

When we listen to the comforts of our hearts, we can focus on the positive progress that has been made to improve the lives of animals. We live in a time now when most people in this country view their pets as family members. The number of organizations helping animals has increased tremendously in this country, and worldwide, over the past three decades. We must remind ourselves that we can only do what we are able to lovingly do at any given moment where we find ourselves faced with heartbreaking situations. Following the animals' ability to unconditionally love, can we extend some compassion to the people who we see as being thoughtless toward animals? We may consider understanding where they are in their own life's journey, and find ways to educate them about the value of animals. And then, as our balancing strategies have taught us, we do as much as we can, letting go afterward but continuing to live in the joy that we so easily give to and receive from animals.

LISTENING TO THE VOICE OF ALL OUR HEARTS

There is nothing that can be said that will lead those who give to animals to conclude, "Well, we have saved some. That will have to be good enough." We will not settle for anything less than helping ALL of the animals; we want to continue to strive toward our vision of a better world for all living beings. The compassion we feel in our hearts can be the catalyst in our striving to work together with others who share our passion, rather than running ourselves ragged and useless. We are not alone. We see and read the stories on the Internet; we talk with fellow animal rights and animal welfare volunteers and workers at conferences and in our neighborhoods. Other like-minded individuals are with us and can offer both emotional and practical support. We can join forces, working together in united hearts and aligned spirits.

One of the most healing aspects of the Giving Heart Retreat at Best Friends Animal Sanctuary every year is the connections that are formed when participants meet for the first time, and find they share many of the same experiences and feelings of the heart. We are reminded that we are all in this together, sometimes facing new challenges that we can best handle with each other's help and support.

Whether we are talking with a fellow animal advocate in person, or simply connecting to their spirit with empathy and respect, at any moment support can make all the difference as we take that next step forward on our journey.

CHAPTER VIII
BALANCING STRATEGY: LIVE

Compassionate toward yourself, you reconcile all beings in the world.

- Tao Te Ching

LIVE FULLY: TAKE CARE OF YOU AND MAKE SPACE

If I were asked to state the most important message of this book, I would choose those ten words above, so eloquently written in Lao Tzu's *Tao Te Ching*. If I were only allowed to share one piece of advice as to how to best help animals, it would be those same ten words. To make *your* difference in the world, begin within. And begin with one moment at a time. It is only by living fully yourself that you are able to be your best as your purpose in the world naturally unfolds. Simply stated, be who you are as best you can in each moment. And how do you do that? Consider the following question as you approach each moment in your life: What is my true heart's desire, now? Then follow through with the answer you receive. Allow your inner wisdom to consider all aspects of the moment at hand: your personal needs, your desires to give, and the conditions of the situation that is presenting itself. You will experience a balance within and a continual and ever-changing flow of giving to and from the heart. Each choice made from this deeper place of compassionate self-care allows you to best give your gifts each moment. It is as simple as that.

PERSONAL STORY

I began to think about writing this chapter while sitting at my kitchen table and sharing fresh steamed vegetables with my dogs. Dressed in my most comfortable shirt and sweatpants, I gazed out the window at a striking autumn view of the foliage in my backyard. I took in the fresh aroma of the rainfall and the beauty of the sky at dusk. Also in view, however, were piles of papers in need of filing, dirty dishes in the sink, litter boxes that needed to be cleaned, and a list of people I needed to call back. So with all of those options of things to do, I asked myself, "What are my true heart's desires, now? " The answer was clear. Feeling comfortable, replenished, and energized, I wanted to write. Although I had previously experienced a two-month writer's block, the words were flowing as I came to the realization that my experience at that moment was an example of the lesson I was about to write about: Take care of you now. I had simply chosen the activity that was speaking to my heart's desire at that moment, and whatever it was that was in the way of my writing flow vanished. I realized that when I fought my need for compassionate self-care in my attempts to force myself to write, the pressure that I created for myself blocked my flow of thoughts. It was only when I let go of my struggle to write and met my own needs, one moment at a time, that I became realigned with the natural flow of energy present in that moment. Becoming aware of and respecting all that is present, including your mood, feelings, surroundings, ideas, environment, etc., is the first step to allowing your natural best to emerge. Then allow that moment to be the best that it can be. And what more could we do than that? Living fully means taking in each experience from a place of replenishment where you have the space in your heart to hear and balance its needs and desires.

TAKE IT FROM FAITH

For years, each day I fed and took care of hundreds of dogs in Dogtown. Afterward I would come home and tackle a house full of my own dogs and cats, then tend to the rabbits, guinea pigs, chickens, turkeys, and sheep. Yes, I said sheep. In the early days of Best Friends, I ended up taking care of the animals that came under the heading "other," meaning any creature that did not seem to fit anywhere else.

As if that weren't enough, at night I would open up a newly published, brightly colored magazine called *Animal's Voice*. *Animal's Voice* was mostly about animal rights and all the ways in which animals were badly treated and abused for food, clothing, sport, and entertainment. As I read the magazine, I would start to feel guilty that I was not doing more to oppose the circus, the zoo, the factory farms, the use of animals in medical experiments, or the use of fur in the fashion industry. It was endless and overwhelming. When we open up and start to see the world from the animals' viewpoint, it is hard ever to close that door again. It can bring about a feeling of helplessness. That's how I felt. Sure, I could do my work helping to take care of abandoned and unwanted dogs, but who was going to fight for the caged bears in China?

Sound familiar? Many of us get into this place where we're miserable that we can't do more. The sheer volume and universality of the problem can overtake our minds and render us ineffective. And what we want most is to be effective on behalf of the animals we love so much. I took myself in hand. Seriously. It was like I was talking to the child within who was hurting badly. I told her to put down the magazine. There were other people taking care of the bears and the cows and the circus animals. And yes, there were ads for secondhand pets in the *Pioneer Shopper*, our free ad paper, but other people would step up to adopt those animals. It's a big world and there are many people helping the animals. You just do your bit. I listened to that parent in me who had stepped up to help my child within and obeyed. I began to focus on the here and now—what was in front of me—in a calmer and more mindful way. At the time, I didn't know that I was starting to practice mindfulness. But that's exactly what I was doing. I had a big job to do at Dogtown. And to do it well I needed to be present and in the moment. As soon as I made that decision, the tensions went away. I had begun to take care of myself.

Karen Martiny, founder of The Animal Rescue of the Rockies in Colorado, learned her lessons on how to live life fully from her first dog Buffy. Buffy suffered a ruptured disc and was paralyzed, requiring a cart to get around. "She's my inspiration," Karen told me. "She lived life to the fullest. Despite her disability, she was sweet, friendly, and fun to go out with. If she could be like that, then so could I," Karen said. But Karen knew, coming from a business background, that she needed more support to get anything done. She discovered one way to take care of herself was to learn to delegate work that needed to be done to others. At the same time she lightened her load, she also taught the new people who came aboard to help animals to also take care of themselves. She taught them how to delegate, too:

> Delegation is the key. It's hard to let go, especially at the start of a new project. But I knew I needed

> help. I created positions: Dog Division Director, Cat Division Director, foster and adoption coordinator, event coordinator, and someone to be in charge of fundraising. These were all volunteer positions. . . . It was important to me to teach self-care to my volunteers from the beginning. I would not allow people to take on too much. I had seen from volunteering at other animal rescue groups how damaging it was when people took on more than they could handle, and burned out. . . .

Karen's understanding of the importance of taking care of herself and maintaining a healthy relationship with her husband not only helped her to become her best, but allowed her to put her strength into action and develop a growing, successful, and healthy organization.

TAKE CARE OF YOURSELF!

Consider the following ten ways to take care of yourself now:

1. **Take a break**, now; don't wait until you feel that you have earned it. Of course, it is fine to reward yourself with a special treat when you have completed a task that you set out to do. Can you go one step further and enjoy a spontaneous gift to yourself before you have even embarked on the task at hand? So go ahead and sit in a comfortable chair and listen to your favorite music before you even start to clean the litter boxes or sort through your piles of bills. An unearned act of self-care is a powerful message to yourself that your personal needs matter. These actions are replenishing and naturally enhance the authentic flow of giving from your heart. For example, the spontaneous self-care that I gave to myself tonight

unexpectedly helped me get past my inability to write.

2. **Become thoughtless in the moment.** Dismiss the excess thoughts. When possible, do not even let them enter your mind when you see them coming. Ask yourself, "Is this thought what I really want or need in this present moment?" You will be surprised how many times your answer will be "No." You truly can choose to think the thoughts that you want to think, rather than the ones that are trying to think you! Try it. Next time you are enjoying a quiet moment with your dog or cat and your mind begins to think about something that brings you stress or unhappiness, question your need to be thinking that thought and send it on its way. Ask yourself, "Is this thought worth taking away my joy or peace of mind?" Embrace the moment at hand without the thoughts of what happened in the past, what you should be doing now, or what you need to do tomorrow. Those self-judgments only detract from the pure joy available to you. And if the thoughts do not seem to leave at your command, allow them to pass through your mind without believing them and letting them influence your mood or actions. As these thoughts lose their power, you can absorb all that the present moment has to offer.

I remember talking to my friend who was struggling to decide whether she should take in a cat who had been abandoned outside her apartment, or bring the cat to an animal shelter. She knew that since the cat was shy and fearful, the cat might do better in a home setting rather than in a shelter. So she decided to foster her. My friend told me that her worries about her ability to find a good home for her feline friend kept her awake at night and added anxiety to her days. Concerned that there are so many cats in need, she found herself repeatedly questioning whether anybody would take a shy cat when they could just as easily find a more outgoing cat to adopt. Her worries escalated and she imagined that this cat might stay hidden when people would come over to see her. Then her thoughts suggested to her that she may not be able to find any home for this cat and she worried what she would do then. But the thoughts didn't stop there. Adding to growing concerns about the future, was the idea that she and the cat might get too attached to each other making it very hard to give her up even if she was eventually able to find a home. And what if she still had the cat when she was needing to be out of town? Since my friend had already brought the cat into her home at that point, all of these worries about the future came crashing in, and they offered nothing helpful to her: only fears and worries. Regardless of how bleak the outcome might be, she was already committed to keeping the cat with her until she found her a home. After many phone calls in which I listened to her repeat her multiple concerns, one day I simply said to her "Don't forget to enjoy this cat now." Those words were all it took for my friend to realize that her worries about the future combined with her negative "what if" thoughts were blocking the natural joy that was available to her now with this loving furry friend in need. She called me a couple of weeks later to let me know that when she remembered to enjoy the cat, she did. She made a deliberate effort to turn off the litany of worries and negativity and focus on enjoying the cat in the present. Much to my friend's surprise, this abandoned cat charmed the first potential adopter who came for a visit; and it was only three weeks later from the time that my friend took her in that she was happily settled in her new family's home.

3. **Put aside your list of things to do.** Don't let it continually play in your brain like a broken record. Do you tend to have long lists on paper or in your head that enumerate things that you must get done? Learn to live with the freedom to have fun in the moment even though you might have a lengthy list of things to do that you have not yet finished. You do not need to wait until your tasks

are complete to enjoy yourself. To execute this strategy, some people find they need to write their list of things to do on a piece of paper so they know that they can always check back and look on it as needed. Others find it easier to not write down the list, but to dismiss it in their minds, and just take things as they come, one at a time.

4. **Ask, "What do I need to do for myself now?"** even when you are in the midst of a task. For example, if you feel like it, stop and take a break even though you are only half finished with the mass mailing or cleaning kennels. For much of my life, I rewarded myself with some act of self-nurturing only after I got all my jobs completely done. I have since found the replenishing value in a "midway through tasks" kind of break. Not only is the time away from the task enjoyed, but I find the second half of the work I am doing to be much more pleasurable after being rejuvenated.

5. **Follow the rhythm and preferences of your body, mind, and soul.** This also means allowing yourself to be less active on days in which your body seems to need replenishing. Perhaps an idea needs to germinate. Your creative juices need some time to flow. A natural rhythm is a tough thing to fight. Sleep longer. Stop and ask, "Where do I feel natural energy?" Perhaps you are in the mood for some physical, mindless activity. On the other hand, if you listen to your natural rhythm, you may find that the last thing you want to do is some form of physical labor and instead you feel you are on the verge of writing a poem. Listen to what you intuitively feel. Don't be afraid to give yourself "a lazy day." Don't answer the phone if you are finding it particularly aversive. Let it go to voicemail and answer it tomorrow. You know if you had an emergency pet or person to attend to, you would let whatever else you had planned to do that day wait—and you wouldn't think poorly about yourself. Maybe you are the emergency, but you don't have to be "an emergency" to give yourself a

break. These are the tricks that help us be our best as we give from a replenished heart.

In addition to your natural rhythm, consider your preferences in the moment before embarking on a specific project. Being in a frame of mind to create a brochure or adoption flyer is a different feeling from the mood for walking dogs or making phone calls. We all know there is always a countless number of options for productive work for our animals, so pay attention to your feelings and choose a task that matches your true inclination at that moment. In addition to finding more pleasure in the undertaking, you are likely to find that the work itself seems to flow with more ease and efficiency.

6. **Save "now" for later.** Keep a notebook of self-care ideas handy that you continually update. The more our minds fill up with to-do lists, the easier it is to forget about the other ways we can show ourselves compassionate self-care. So when you get an urge to nurture yourself in some way, and you cannot indulge it on the spot, write the idea down in your notebook. When you read or hear about an appealing treat or relaxing activity jot it down with the intention of experiencing it at another time. Keep your notebook handy so at a moment's notice you can choose an act of self-care that uniquely meets your present need.

7. **Incorporate self-care into each act of giving now.** When you are about to begin a chosen task ask yourself, "How can I make it as enjoyable as possible?" For example, if it is on your list to travel some distance, choose a time of day with less traffic that will give you a more pleasant trip. Consider bringing an animal or human friend along and music that you especially enjoy. I used to try to clear out my days when my nephews or nieces were staying with me, but then discovered that so many of the Blessed Bonds tasks were more enjoyable when they came along with me. Supportive of my endeavors, they were open to experiencing the new adventure of being a part of

those tasks, too.

8. **Focus on the present joy**. Recently my nephew found a mamma cat, a papa cat and four kittens together in a small carrier that was abandoned in the tall grass of an empty lot. When I first received the call from him my mind immediately became flustered and anxious. What would I do? How would I find them homes? Where will we keep them? Who should I call? When I went to meet the precious family of kitties who had been abandoned I sat still with myself for a moment to tell myself my own advice that I had given my friend when she took in an abandoned cat: "Don't forget to find the joy." I reminded myself that my tendency to love and adore new animals in need, within seconds of meeting them, was a blessing. This natural ability allows me to let them touch my soul and bring me peace, laughter, and love. If I filled my mind only with worry and angst, I would block that natural joy that was available to me as a person who naturally gives and receives from the animals. So in telling myself to find the joy *now*, I did. Cuddling the kittens in my arms gave me a sense of peace that quieted the frantic worries of my mind. I intuitively knew that everything would be all right, taking it one step at a time as I have done so many times in the past. But I had to make the decision to find the joy in the moment at hand and allow it to overrule the angst.

9. **Build on the natural joy that the present moment already contains**. When everything feels great feel it. Take in all that this moment in life has to offer. Don't be afraid to enjoy for fear that such happiness cannot continue. When I am at Best Friends Animal Sanctuary I take pleasure in every soul-nourishing aspect of the experience. I dismiss the thoughts that count how many days of my trip are finished and how few are left. I make it a point to remind myself to look for the beauty and enjoy the peace and not take any of it for granted. I focus on each one of my senses to fully take it all in; I observe, I

listen, I feel, I smell, and I taste. I feel the gratitude for the chance to be there. I allow myself to feel this wonderfully small and protected feeling I get surrounded by massive canyons. I let my imagination drift to all the people who have walked there before and all who will enjoy the place after me. I feel surrounded by loving animals and people who love animals. What more could I ask for? It's a piece of heaven. With all the excitement of the workshops and the new people I will meet, I do not want to miss this amazing natural replenishment that awaits me upon every arrival. As beautiful as the sunny skies can be, I remember an especially enjoyable day during a rare blizzard when I happened to be in Kanab (the home of Best Friends Animal Sanctuary). Whatever the moment brings is mine to savor.

10. **Enjoy your own furry family now**. As seasoned animal folk, we learn too quickly that these beloved friends will not be with us as long as we wish they could be. This realization can take us out of the present moment we have with each of them. The worries and anticipation of their illness and eventual death can get in the way of our full experience of the bond. Give away your heart. Let them give to you all that they have to give in the moment at hand. Take the time to spend quality time with your own animals. Watch them, cuddle them, feel the sense of blessing you have for getting to be the one who shares their life's journey. Don't miss out on the joy by attempting to protect your vulnerable heart. Open yourself to the vast power of the soulful bond.

MAKE SPACE

After being consumed by animal rescue myself and talking with thousands of animal advocates over the years, I discovered the importance of physical, mental, and emotional space in one's life; it is essential to have space so that acts of self-care have a place to occur and grow. I found it hard to resist filling any empty spaces in my everyday life, especially when there was a chance to do something to help an animal, which there always is. There were already more things that I wanted to do to help animals than was possible. So I eliminated space: the few minutes to lie in bed in the morning before facing the day, sleep, time to read before bed, zoning out in a chair. Every activity overlapped with the next so when an unplanned event would occur I immediately felt helplessly stressed because there was no place to put the new demand. There was no space for me to consider what my heart's true desires were at any given moment—every moment was already filled in. It wasn't until I cleared some space that I was able even to begin to recognize and nurture the needs of my own heart.

Do you need to take that first step and create space so you can recognize your unique needs and actively practice the daily self-care that will allow you to live and give fully? Leaving room for compassionate acts toward yourself allows them to find their way into your life naturally. If you do not know where to begin to nurture yourself, begin by creating and preserving emptiness. Leave some physical, mental, and emotional space unfilled. Are you in need of some space? Consider these ten ways to begin making space in your life:

1. **Have non-animal time in your life.** Even if you think you do not need it, perhaps your friends and family would appreciate it! You may have forgotten about other hobbies and interests that you enjoy alone as well as those that are fun with family and friends. Give yourself some time to explore the possibilities.

2. **Allow open "in case of an emergency" time every week.** One of the things most stressful about a crisis is not having time for it. Recently, my beloved Chilidog needed dental surgery. I scheduled it when I was able to be home for two days following the surgery. He had fourteen teeth removed, and being a senior dog, it was a rough recovery. What a difference it made to have left that space open to be with him and know that I had the time to give him whatever he needed, without canceling clients or juggling responsibilities. I felt so much more at peace about facing whatever challenges were presented because I left the space open to be fully available. Looking back, I am sure that the peaceful energy that I felt was much more conducive to his healing than what my state of mind would have been had I planned to keep up my usual schedule of busy work activity. No emergencies occurred so this extra gift of space made our time together during his recovery that much more enjoyable.

3. **Make space by removing some of your own expectations.** Responsible people know how to get things done. Some people write daily lists on paper, others have reminders programmed into their cellphones. Routines may be followed to ensure certain procedures are carried out. Think about your self-expectations for the past few days. Did you have tasks that you wanted to get done that you turned into a rule for the day? Have you ever had your list of things to do in the car with you and felt the resistance of just not wanting to do those last three tasks? What would it be like to go ahead and skip them for the day? I know that once I have written down the names and phone numbers of calls to return on a given day, it is hard for me to let myself wait until the next day to complete the task I had planned to finish. My tentative plans often turn into rules that I then must follow. For example, if I get the notion to buy dog treats on a given day and then I don't, it can feel like a broken rule rather than a choice or a change

of plans. Sometimes you can make that extra space you need by simply asking yourself how necessary the rule that you made for yourself really is. Next time you make your list for the day, whether it's the old fashioned way of writing it down or an electronic reminder, try taking something off the list before you even begin the day!

4. **Create space by remembering that sometimes good enough is enough.** Did you grow up with the mantra "Just do your best?" That simple statement can cause a lot of stress until we add a clause: "Do your best given all the circumstances at the time." We create space when we lower our own self-expectations. Sometimes good enough is enough. Perhaps if you stayed up until two o'clock in the morning, the brochure would be a little better. But could it also be good enough as is and be more important for you to get your sleep? Or better yet maybe somebody else could even create the brochure! It may not be as perfect as it could be if you did it, but might it not be good enough? When finding your healthy balance in life, you may need to let go of some of those ideal expectations you have placed on yourself. There will always be more we want to do for our furry friends than we can ever do.

5. **Consider putting extra space between a request for help and your response.** Ask yourself if you are in the best state of mind to listen to messages. I used to feel quite anxious and overwhelmed when I listened to messages at ten o'clock at night from the Blessed Bonds' voicemail after working a full day in my psychology practice. I was much more able to think clearly and relate compassionately when I waited and returned calls after a good night's sleep.

But your own state of mind is not the only reason to provide space between a request and a response. Although space is defined as nothingness, it has a very powerful effect on the unfolding of life events. Space allows others to realize that they may have the answer to the question they are putting to you. When you respond to a request for help with some space you are telling the asker that you believe they may hold the answers to their own question. Recently, I gave space to the request of a person who wanted me to call her immediately and pick up two kittens that she had taken in and were doing their business outside of the litter box. I was on my way out of town, knew that I was not in a position to take her two kittens, and also was confident in her abilities to step back and resolve the situation. A few weeks later, I received an adorable video of her two kittens with her daughter. They had become family members and there was no mention of any litter box problems. Having spent so many years in direct animal rescue work, Faith also relays countless stories of issues that were resolved by the callers after some time had passed before their phone call or email was returned. Without words, allowing space may give the message that the requester has the ability to solve their own problem with the animal at hand.

6. **Consider putting space between someone else's negativity directed at you.** If you receive a message that someone is angry with you or perhaps is registering a complaint against you or your organization, can you step back, sleep on it, and give it some space? Consider not responding quickly to an email with the same anger that's being directed at you. Perhaps you feel compelled to write a response. Can you put it in the draft folder for a few hours and get back to it?

7. **Create space when you cannot find an answer.** With space present, insight has a place to emerge and creative problem solving has a chance to flow in an uncluttered mind and a replenished body. Don't problems feel more manageable on a good night's sleep? Have you ever had that experience where an answer to a problem suddenly comes into your mind after you let it go? New ideas need a place to blossom. In an article published in *Best Friends*

Magazine, a board president remarks about how the empty space she opened for taking care of herself is where she found a $200,000 answer to her shelter's needs. She views that space as what saved the organization, which in turn saved countless animals' lives.

Personal Story: Sometimes the answer suddenly emerges when you stop the incessant effort to find it. I experienced this phenomenon with my particularly intuitive cat, Eddie. He was a senior cat of mine who had undergone surgery to have tumors in his ears removed. A few days later, test results came back indicating that he had an aggressive form of cancer, explaining his difficult and slow recovery. It was the following morning after receiving this sad report that Eddie awoke at six in the morning, in significant distress. Anxiously, I weighed my options; I wanted to get him help, but knew that my vet, who had come to love Eddie in spite of his unpredictable ways, would not be open for another hour. I hesitated taking Eddie to the emergency room as he could become very unmanageable in unknown settings. To add to the stress in deciding what to do, my mother-in-law had stayed at our house overnight so I could take her to a doctor's appointment in the morning. Feeling anxious, upset, and panicked I was not sure what to do. Should I pick him up and put him in the car and wait for my vet to open or go the closest emergency room? Should I cancel my mother-in-law's doctor appointment? Should I get my husband out of the shower to help? In my anxious state, I could not determine the best choice to make for Eddie. At that moment, I felt an intuitive message from Eddie to just let it be, and to go sit on the couch in the living room with him. I felt a sudden sense of peace because I felt that on some level, I was doing what Eddie wanted me to do. Within fifteen minutes, Eddie passed away peacefully in my arms that were now attached to the calm body that had let go of the stress. When I emptied my mind of all the noise in my head and home that morning the space was there for me to hear what Eddie and I truly needed, and I was in a place to give it to him.

8. **Make space for your own furry family.** Carve out time for you to spend time with your own family of pets. Allow them to feel what you need, and let them provide it for you. Let them make you laugh. Take walks and naps with them by your side. Although you love all of the animals that cross your path and are under your care, keep yourself nourished with furry family time. I know for me there is something very comforting about going back to my own family of pets after busily checking on everybody else under my care. Quite often I bring one of my dogs along for the ride when I am picking up another pet in need, or engaging in some kind of activity related to my rescue work. I enjoy bringing Chilidog to work as my therapy assistant. He provides therapy to my clients as well as to me. Even the demands of keeping their vet appointments feel like time set aside for my own family. Carve out family bonding time that you enjoy, and don't forget the humans!

Personal Story: After my fifteen-year-old dog Lukas passed away in 2006, my husband and I had thought that we were plenty busy with the Blessed Bonds foster pets and decided we would not adopt any more pets of our own. Lukas was the last of our challenging terriers to pass away, and only Fritzi, our sweet senior dog, and a few intermittent fosters filled a house that had previously been home to seven dogs. The decision not to adopt any more of our own lasted for two months. With only well-behaved dogs in the house, we both felt the void. Along came Milo, a Westie with an attitude, and quite a few issues that we attributed to his homeless days living in a car. And then two foster dogs, Teddy and Jack, were added to the mix; all three shared those endearing challenges that one might expect from three rambunctious male terrier mixes. My husband and I both knew that they were here to stay, and the void was filled as the "Harper-Gallo Home for Wayward Furry Boys" was back in full swing again. All was right with the world. We had learned that we should never sacrifice the joy of having our own family of pets in order to save all the pets of the world. Being heroic didn't have to mean being deprived.

9. **Keep space in your mind.** Incessant thinking—one thought after another—is a common source of stress. Thinking can take on a force of its own. Can you become thoughtless? Can you choose to not think and create an emptiness, a void of thought in your mind? Can you replace your thoughts with empty space or a visual image of a spacious scene—an ocean, the sky—places where your thoughts can dissolve? There are a variety of meditative practices out there; experiment and see what works for you.

10. **Listen with space.** Space has its place in our relationship with others. When you begin to communicate with another person, clear out your pre-conceived notions about how the conversation will go. Make space in your mind to truly listen to what the other has to say. When your mind starts to form your next sentence while the other person is still talking, dismiss it so that you can continue to listen with your full, unclouded attention. Allow that space to continue to present itself until you feel truly ready to respond from a place of calmness and understanding.

THE EFFECTS OF LIVING FULLY

As the *Tao Te Ching* so wisely tells us, the compassion that we give to ourselves reconciles all beings in the world. To live fully is not a luxury that you can afford only every once in a while, but is your personal responsibility so that you can effectively do your part in the world. Positive energy matters. People who give themselves what they need radiate a positive and joyful presence that other living beings can sense. Do the people and pets in your life deserve experiencing the best part of you, someone who is fun, interesting, and enjoyable to be around? At the same time, you will attract more people to your cause because your joy will be contagious. Most importantly, however, when you allow yourself to fully live, you take a step forward for all living beings. Begin within, and your influence on the animals, others, and the world will expand naturally with infinite possibilities.

CHAPTER IX
THE GIFTS OF THE JOURNEY

There are always gifts available to us in life; we simply need to be open to them. Last week, I mistakenly brought a pre-paid UPS package to FedEx instead of UPS. While I was in the store, I saw a particular printer cord on the clearance table that was exactly what I had been looking for at half the usual price. This lucky find occurred only because I had walked into the wrong store. I took this instance as an obvious reminder that there are gifts in everything. Sometimes, however, the gifts are not as easy to find as my printer cord was, especially in more challenging life situations. Even amidst the frustration, sadness, and disappointment that life may bring, there are always gifts available to us.

Just by their very nature, animals seem to make it easier to find these everyday gifts. For one thing, they provide unconditional love and support to us as life sends its challenges. They are a comforting and dependable constant in our lives. Their unexpected antics can bring laughter and joy and in simply caring for them we find the gifts of meaningfulness and purpose. Unlimited affection and companionship are standard. Even scientific research confirms what animal lovers have always known: the presence of pets speeds up recovery from surgery, lowers blood pressure, and decreases depression. Studies conclude that living with pets enhances our overall emotional and physical wellbeing. In addition to bringing us these simple pleasures, our animal friends model for us how to find the gifts in everything. For example, a cat goes with the flow when he turns a room full of boxes into an exciting maze, or a dog finds an old towel to be the perfect place for a nap. They teach us how to enjoy the small stuff, laugh at ourselves, embrace the present moment, savor food, forgive, and even how to handle illness and death. Their gifts also help us better help them as they lead us to two life-changing discoveries: 1) our *best selves*, our true essence guided by *inner wisdom,* and 2) our collective power, what happens when our *best selves* connect with others to make a difference for the animals.

THE DISCOVERY OF YOUR *BEST SELF*

You do not need to create inner wisdom; it has been with you all along. Learning to let it guide your life, however, may be an ongoing practice. Your *best self* takes charge of your journey when the obstructing thoughts that interfere with its natural flow are removed. This *best self* exists within each and every one of us, awaiting discovery. Michelangelo has often been credited with saying that every block of marble contains a perfect statue that is revealed when the imprisoning walls around it are removed. Similarly, your *best self* emerges when you strip away the limiting thoughts that detract from the fullness of life offered to you at each moment. When your *best self* leads the way there is a natural flow to your life that you can't miss.

PERSONAL STORY

Abundance of joy is just there for the taking as I

experienced this past year on my fifty-fifth birthday. I opened my eyes that morning with excitement; I was going to spend the morning with Emma and Sammy, two senior dogs who had been brought to an animal control facility by a distraught and homeless owner who had to be hospitalized. The first time I met them had been three weeks before, and I remembered it well. I'd been struck by the immense love I felt from them instantly. I had the most delightful day those three weeks back; most of our time together was spent in the car. We went to the pet groomer, the veterinarian at the shelter, a pet supply store, and finally to my home for the evening. I felt unconditional love from them to a degree I had never before experienced! Was this because these were the two most affectionate, loving, and appreciative dogs ever to cross my path? Did I believe that they were able to express love more than any other animal I have ever met in all my thirty years of rescue work and fifty-five years on Earth? I don't think so. While they were certainly wonderful companions for the day, it was I who was different. Because I was open to the gifts of the journey that day I was able to receive the boundless love and immense joy that was available to me. I now know that these kinds of extraordinary gifts in our ordinary days are always present. On this particular day, my *best self* was in charge and thus able to welcome it all in. I felt energized, peaceful, supported, and loved. I felt love pouring out of me. I knew that I was exactly where I needed to be and delighted in each moment of the day. I didn't even know at the time that this fun and invigorating day would become an inspiring story in a presentation that I would give a week later on the need for, and rewards of, fostering pets whose families are in crisis.

When I awoke on the morning of my birthday I was bubbling over with anticipatory excitement at spending some time with my two canine buddies again who had brought me so much love and happiness just three weeks prior. And once again the day brought all kinds of unexpected delights, beginning with a tremendously loving and affectionate welcome from Emma and Sammy. What was different this time, however, was that this unconditional love and acceptance that I felt from and toward the dogs seemed to extend to everybody and everything that I encountered all day. The dogs were once again full of love and seemed to find delight in everything around them. These feelings were contagious, and I found myself in love with life and enjoying everything about the day. I spontaneously bought and delivered doughnuts to the animal shelter where the dogs were going for a vet check-up and I felt a strong sense of gratitude from the staff and volunteers for the unexpected treats. A wave of admiration for their hard work and dedication came over me. As strange as this might sound, I even felt a connection to the people at the grocery store. I had an enjoyable exchange with the cashier who told me I had won a tote bag for simply being there at that moment. The slow traffic did not bother me in the least, and the music playing on my favorite radio station never sounded so beautiful. The fresh pear that I ate for a snack was juicy and scrumptiously delicious. I felt especially high on life at that moment, a peaceful yet enthusiastic and energetic contentment; all was well with the world.

So what does it take for our *best selves* to emerge and open us up to all the gifts that await our discovery on our unique journey with the animals? As an animal advocate, you know that your life's purpose will always include the desire to love and help animals; that path is already carved into your heart. But to what extent will you receive and enjoy all that your acts of giving to the animals offer you? Unlimited gifts are available to you. Removing the thoughts that block their flow will allow you to receive them. And, of course, it begins within with the simple commitment to balance your own needs with the desires you have to help the animals. This promise to yourself is the key to unlocking the peace of mind, the joy, and the deep contentment that underlie this journey and await you every single day. And you will have more to give to the animals. Not only do we learn how to live from a deeper place through the natural loving bond the animals form with us, but they actually help us become our *best selves*. We become better able to help them so they in turn are better able to help us and the infinite spiral keeps rising.

A Peaceful Aliveness

Jan, a sixty-year-old lifetime animal lover and advocate who works in a rescue-oriented dog and cat boarding facility, reported the following experience on New Year's Day:

> As I was sitting in a chair in my living room with my cats surrounding me, I suddenly and unexpectedly felt pure contentment about where I am right now, today. I felt no regrets or resentments for anything that had happened before today; I realized that it all led up to where I am now. I knew that all of my life experiences including the jobs that had disappointed me, had led me to this moment, one of complete peace and joy like I have not felt before. I realized it was the animals. Being around them gave me that sense of peace. I am so happy. It's a quiet feeling. I am enveloped with peace. I feel no resentment about the difficulties that led up to now—they are part of what makes this moment what it is now. This feeling is timeless; the past doesn't matter, nor does whatever happens from here. The animals have healed me and it is from a very deep place inside of me. It cannot be taken away; their love is there forever, as is my love for them.

So what are these guiding forces so naturally displayed by the animals that lead us to rediscover our *best selves?* In my own contemplations and writings over the past twenty years, I find there to be three forces guiding us to our *best self*, the "me" that's directed by natural inner wisdom. It is these guiding forces that not only bring joy to our everyday lives, but also allow us to offer our best gifts to animals, other people, and the world. It is not surprising to me that they are continually revealed in the natural way that our animal companions relate to us. I refer to these three forces as "The Three As": Authenticity, Acceptance, and Appreciation.

1. **Authenticity.** Experiencing life with authenticity means recognizing who you really are. Your true self guides your daily actions, and the gifts that you share with the world are aligned with your natural talents and strengths. You are aware of your vulnerabilities and know which of your buttons can be pushed into reactions that will temporarily block this innate wisdom. Authenticity means learning what you need to do in order to nurture and replenish yourself, and then honoring those discoveries in the everyday choices that you make.

The animals show us how to live according to the principle of authenticity and they naturally support us in those actions that follow their lead. They are true to their own natures and thereby bring out our own natural essence. Our animal friends don't even know how to be any different from whom they are and so we exhibit the same behavior in response. Have you ever felt that you needed to put on airs or be someone that you are not while with your animals? It is hard to be superficial in the presence of our animal friends. They unconditionally love us, and allow us to use that love to strengthen our own self-confidence. They support us in letting that true self shine through with them and with others. A shared realization was expressed by many of those with whom I spoke to after Hurricane Katrina: "I never knew I had it in me." They were referring to how their own personal strengths seemed to emerge when they were rescuing animals from the floods. They were able to problem solve and persevere in ways they never had before in their lives. They described themselves as "courageous" and "holding strong." One rescuer told me that she felt that if she could handle all that she saw, she now knew she could handle anything that life brought her and that it was a gift that came from such a tragedy.

2. **Acceptance.** Living with acceptance means taking in all that life offers without resistance, even those experiences that you label as unpleasant or bad. While you may not like an action you see or even condone it, your *best self* chooses to surrender to what is. Guided by acceptance, you are challenged to experience events that you did not choose, do not want, and sometimes may even think that you cannot handle.

Acceptance means taking the moment in exactly as it is. There is no doubt that our animal friends are some of the greatest life teachers and role models for accepting what the moment brings. I remember noting how well Jess, my blind dog, dealt with his inability to hold himself up when he suffered from a sudden vestibular imbalance. Jess simply and naturally lay down in a comfortable spot on the grass in the sun. He seemed perfectly accepting that he wasn't able to run down the hill as he clearly had planned to do just a few moments earlier. Instead, he waited for me to come and sit down next to him, and wagged his tail and greeted me with a lick as usual. With no appearance of panic or discomfort, he responded to his feelings in the moment and embraced what the moment offered with ease and surrender. So often animals seem to accept what is going on in any given moment and just go with the flow. Have you experienced a dog that will get up in the night with you at the very first inkling that you are moving, with no indication that you have disrupted his sleep? You are up, so he is up—simple as that. And the gift he receives is extra time with you. Time and time again, our animal friends show us that when you accept what is the gifts of that moment are naturally revealed.

In addition to being role models for acceptance, it is often the animals in our lives who naturally present us with the opportunities to find the peace and joy that this acceptance brings to life experiences, even the most challenging ones. It was a participant of the pet loss support group who described a "welcomed and much needed transformation in her life" during the last year of her dog's terminal illness. She believed that it stressed out her dog when he sensed that his human companion was upset. In her determination to give him the best possible day every day, she knew she needed to stop anticipating the future and fully stay in the present moment. She knew that he was not obsessing over his cancer, but continuing fully to enjoy each day as it came. She took his lead and decided to focus fully on their time left, however much there might be. Of course, she wished he did not get sick, but she believed that it was when she fully accepted and faced this terminal illness as part of their journey that she found peaceful clarity in every decision. She chose to slow her life down and take more time to enjoy his favorite things with him, like walks in the woods and playing ball. She described the realization she had when she only took whatever challenge arose throughout their time together, one moment at a time, and trusted herself to do the best she could. With just one decision at a time, she could hold onto that peace. She shared with the group how grateful she was for her special bond, and that she believed her dog's demonstration of accepting each moment as it came has lead her to a peace in her heart that she never knew could exist and that she would always have from now on. She expressed her eternal gratefulness.

3. **Appreciation.** Experiencing life with appreciation means welcoming the complexities of the human experience as life unfolds. Life happens, but it may not

unfold the way you had hoped it would. Perhaps you expected something to turn out completely different. Your needs and desires may seem to conflict with the conditions of your life. You may find yourself in situations that cause inner turmoil, or require personal strength, empathy, or forgiveness. When you appreciate life's mysteries even painful choices can be a chance to uncover possibilities never before revealed. Interestingly, but not surprising, we can observe these same qualities in the way that animals relate to life, and we can experience them firsthand in our bonds with them.

In the spirit of appreciation, we allow life to unfold. There is no doubt that life's greatest teachers for "going with the flow" are our animal friends. We observe how quickly they adapt to new situations, like showering love on their new foster family, then making their new adoptive family feel like their one and only. They enjoy what the accumulation of life's moments bring. If it rains a lot, the dogs enjoy the mud. When your life gets too busy and your rooms get disorganized, cats aren't concerned about the clutter; they're delightfully intrigued by the stack of boxes and papers that are everywhere. Do your animal friends play with those wadded up pieces of paper that didn't make the wastebasket? They are naturals at finding the hidden gifts in whatever life is offering at that moment. And if we are open to it, they will share that simple sense of pleasure with us. The sharing might be in the form of a tree branch placed at our feet or a wet nose or warm body snuggled up close against our legs bringing us warmth under the covers.

The animals in our lives lead us to appreciate the many turns we take on our journey, often influenced and directed by our bond with them. So many animal advocates with whom I have spoken report stories of how a deep bond with a pet led them on their chosen path of helping animals in some way that is aligned with their natural gifts. For example, in her late teens, my cat's veterinarian changed her career aspirations from home economics education to veterinary medicine after she became involved in the medical treatment of her family dog. She believes that her "true calling" to be of service to animals was realized. It is interesting that her extraordinary talent for and love of sewing developed into her highly acclaimed surgical skills. Our animal friends serve as both role models and integral influences in the often surprising and mysterious unfolding of our life's journey.

As we learn from examples set by animals and our interactions with them, our *best self* naturally emerges as we approach each life experience as we really are, accepting what is, and then appreciating how it all flows together. What more wonderful gift could they offer us than to help us live a life in sync with our *best selves* as we embrace each moment? Animals are amazing. They give us another immeasurable gift. They show us exactly what we need in order to create a better world for animals, the discovery of our collective power to make a difference. Motivated by love and driven by our shared vision to improve their lives, our *best selves* intersect and connect with each other. Living with and learning from our animal friends allows each of us to uncover that natural ability to relate to each other with energy, creativity, and support. It is this unity of spirit and action that is the key to changing the equation of *hearts larger than hands* to *our collective hearts equal to our collective hands*. It is through the influence of our precious bond with the animals that we develop the capacity to unite, each of us directed by our *best selves*. And what could be more natural? Who is better to show us how to help them than the animals themselves? And what greater gift could we receive from them than being shown the way to create a kinder world for all of them, as well as for ourselves? Our vision for a kinder world for all living beings suddenly becomes within our reach.

So how do we then activate our *best selves* to work together for the animals? Begin within. For some people, relating to animals can be much easier than relating to humans. If that's true for you, then perhaps the animals themselves can help guide you on how to use your *best self* in relating to other people for the benefit of animals. Plus, we can always let authenticity, acceptance, and appreciation guide us. When we consider treating each other with even just a small part of the love and understanding that we give and receive from animals, infinite possibilities emerge. Let's revisit the "The Three As" again from the animals' point of view, which reveal the keys to working with each other so we can best help the animals and ourselves.

1. ***Authenticity*** **means: Be who you are with others.**
2. ***Acceptance*** **means: Allow others to be who they are.**
3. ***Appreciation*** **means: Let life do what it does.**

1. Authenticity: **Be who you are with others.** There is no doubt that animals are their true selves. Have you ever seen a furry friend pretend to be something other than what she or he is? We fall in love with this uniqueness, the quirks, and the true essence of their beings. Authenticity is the dog or cat just being who they are without pretense. The animal lover in return feels completely free to be his or her true self with the dog or cat. Sometimes it takes courage for us to be willing to put our authentic selves out there in the world of people. It might mean saying no when you know others are expecting you to say yes. Responding with authenticity may mean that you need to step back from a situation when being in it is preventing you from living in ways consistent with who you are. You may experience the loss of people or things that you had feared losing. But no matter what else happens, our animal friends continue to love and support us for who we really are. They show us how easy it is to just to be ourselves.

So how does being true to ourselves help us help the animals? Conflicts with people are inevitable. Knowing and being who you really are will allow you to stay grounded when these struggles arise. An honest look at who you are in the situation and what you need to do in the spirit of authenticity is the first step to finding resolution. For example, someone coming at you with anger does not mean that you must react back in a similar manner. Take a moment, step back, and let your inner wisdom guide your next response. In working together with others, we simply need to be ourselves—our *best selves*.

2. ***Acceptance:*** **Allow others to be who they are.** Our relationships with animals are an excellent illustration of mutual acceptance; they accept us and we accept them. What a difference it would make in human relationships if we were able to apply our ability to deal with our animals' idiosyncratic traits to our relationships with people! Why can we love our pets, flaws and all, while the humans in our lives are in constant danger of angering us with their imperfections? I can think of my own furry family as an example. My husband and I love Milo, our tough little Westie. Yes, he would bite us if we got too close to his food or treats. We have learned not to startle him from sleep or move our chairs when he has placed himself under them. We do not understand where his impulsive aggression toward us might come from, but we do not take it personally; we work around his less likeable traits and love him all the same. We do the same for Skippy, an older feral cat who now lives with us indoors. We meet his needs and give him the space he needs. We would both love the chance to show Skippy physical affection, but we respect the fact that this does not feel comfortable to him so we refrain from petting him. I am sure you can think of plenty of examples from your own relationships with the animals in your life where you gave them the benefit of the doubt and many, many extra chances. Perhaps, you let go

of your own expectations and defended an animal with a behavior or trait that you would never tolerate in a human. We are not likely to take the animals' eccentricities personally, and we might even enjoy the challenge of finding a way to work around an odd personality trait so that everyone is happy.

My good friends adopted a cat that they adore, knowing she had a history of frequently peeing outside of the box. They recently shared with me what it takes for them to keep that cat consistently using the litter box. It involves a specific way of putting out food, followed by one of them taking a few steps to the right and then to the left, and then the other one singing a song they wrote together that tells the kitty how wonderful she is! They tell the story with both laughter and pride in their life-saving and quite creative "out of the box" problem-solving skills. We freely give our compassion, love, and understanding to these animals. We naturally emphasize the good traits and play down the difficult ones. We see what we can do to make conditions that will allow that animal to be at his or her best. We strive to uncover that *best self* in the animal. What would our relationships with our fellow humans be like if we were able to offer the same kind of acceptance to them? Can you treat that person as if you were relating to their *best self*, even if it is not showing itself in that particular moment?

Acceptance also means that we let go of our need to change others. It cannot be our job since it is not within our power. Change can only come from within. We may not like all that we see, but suspending judgment and seeking to understand is the first step toward a resolution. You may still find that you need to go your different ways. Perhaps, however, you may find that you can accept the difference and still work together, respecting each other's viewpoints and continuing to work together, emphasizing the commonalities that you do share.

Have you heard of the QTIP approach to getting along with others? QTIP stands for Quit Taking It

Personally. When we accept others, just like when we are accepting our furry friends, we realize that each living being responds from their individual personality as well as a whole lifetime of experiences. It is not personal and there is no need for us to take offense. We need only to recognize the action for what it is: their issue based on their experiences, not yours. It is not up to you to fix it. In summary, the second key to working together with others is to show others some of the compassion you so freely give to the animals.

3. ***Appreciation*: Let life do what it does.** Every day we see how animals go with the flow in dealing with us. They accept our moods and the changes in their day-to-day situations, they continue to make the most of whatever life brings. Like us, animals often experience challenges on their life journey: sickness, new homes, new families, and additions and subtractions to their human families throughout their lives. These are just a few common trials for a pet. Overall, they continue to weather the storm, adapting to change and continuing to approach life with love, enthusiasm, and a sense of adventure. In our mutually loving relationships with them, it is easy for us to respond to their particular needs and make adjustments when our relationship to them deems it necessary. For example, a friend of mine keeps her house quiet and the television off, as her cat is sensitive to noise. It did not feel like a sacrifice to her and she has enjoyed the gift of quietness. When we apply the principal of appreciation to our relationships with other humans as well, we allow the complexities, the mysteries, and the surprises in our relationships with people to lead us to new places.

I have known many animal lovers who have not hesitated to remodel their homes to accommodate their pets' needs. A family opened their home to a stray cat that later saved their lives by alerting them to a fire that had broken out in their home. I have heard countless stories of rescue organizations that were formed because of one person's experience with an animal that touched their life. The third key to getting along with others is to let go of your expectations and go with the flow. It can lead to surprising rewards.

So putting it all together, how do we apply these guiding principles when relating to people? Among the multitude of lessons I have received from my animal friends, I would like to share with you the wisdom shown to me by two in particular: Chilidog and Felix the cat. First, let's turn to my wise psychotherapy assistant, Chilidog, whose very being illustrates the way these guiding principles can work together when we relate to others.

A LESSON FROM CHILIDOG

Chilidog is my senior dachshund who was rescued from deplorable living conditions and has been my therapy assistant for the past four years. He interacts with a variety of people and has formed many relationships while working with me at the office. He also accompanies me to most places that I go. He is deeply loved for who he is, a gentle, loving soul. Sometimes he is feeling more energetic than other times; he might greet my client at the door wagging his tail, or snooze in his bed throughout the entire session. In the spirit of acceptance, he takes people for whoever they are and whatever mood they are in. If they want snuggling. he accommodates. If they ignore him, that's fine, too. He helped two younger clients overcome their fear of dogs. Another client tells me that she pictures Chilidog in her mind when she is feeling down. He prefers to be with me most of the time, but enjoys the other dogs at home and cuddles up with my husband when I am out of town. He is himself, he allows others to be who they are, and he goes along with life as it is happening, finding all the gifts that are present.

So how do we follow Chilidog's lead and apply "The Three As" to our interactions in a way that will allow us to work best together to help the animals? Let's start by recalling or imagining a conflict between you and another individual who is involved in animal rescue. Now apply Authenticity, Acceptance, and Appreciation principles. First, take a breath and give yourself some quiet reflection, even if it's for just a moment, and allow your true feelings about the situation to present themselves to you. No matter what anyone else says or how a situation turns out your personal views and values are not threatened and will continue to be at your core. Embracing this reassurance allows you to put your *best self* in charge. Next, accept the challenge of whatever you are facing. You do not have to like it, but just simply realize that it is there right now. What is life asking you to accept? Not forever, only in this moment at hand. Can you approach your fellow advocate with concern and kindness? Are you willing to listen with an open mind, reserve judgment, and seek to understand? If you cannot answer yes to these questions then wait to respond and give yourself a little more time to find that place of love and compassion as you face the challenge at hand. Finally, appreciate that the flow of life includes the natural highs along with the most difficult challenges. Find peace with knowing that you have given the *best self* response that was available to you in that moment and let it go. You will then be ready to experience whatever life brings next with authenticity, acceptance, and appreciation.

A Lesson from Felix

I was privileged to know Felix, a twenty-three-

and-a-half-year-old black cat wise beyond his years, during the last three and a half years of his life when he so naturally and easily illustrated the guiding principles in the way he lived his life. Felix was twenty years old when I first met him. His owner, Arlene, was told by her doctor that she could not continue to live with her beloved friend because her allergies to him were exacerbating her medical condition, resulting in frequent visits to the emergency room. Arlene's daughter brought Felix to the cat vet and sanctuary where I volunteered at that time. Arlene and Felix had been inseparable companions for over twenty years; it was breaking her heart to give him up, and likely it was breaking his, too. Arlene's daughter wondered if Felix could adjust to such a drastic change at his age, or if euthanasia offered a more humane option. But Felix still had much more love to give and to receive. Not only did he adjust and thrive within hours of coming to us, but he continued to prosper during the next three and a half years. Whether or not Felix asked himself the three questions that ensure natural giving or just followed the way to heartfelt giving instinctually, he demonstrated the gifts of the natural flow to and from the heart.

Felix and Authenticity

Felix gave his own way. Felix was true to himself in both honoring his needs and in reaching out to others. He began "lap-hopping" within a few hours of his arrival. Plopping himself on any available lap, he asked for the extra love and attention that he needed so that he could continue with his own giving journey. He cuddled with his fellow felines for catnaps and meowed loudly for his meals and his snacks. A lack of teeth did not seem to interfere with his obvious enjoyment of food of all kinds, and he voraciously devoured every bite. He was himself and we loved him all the more for sharing his big personality with us.

Felix gave of himself with his own unique and irresistible style. One of his trademarks was what we named "full-body hugs." After hopping onto a lap, Felix would wrap his arms around the neck of an unsuspecting fan and squeeze as hard as he could. Given Felix's chronic nasal condition, the adoring human recipient of his gifts would often receive a full wet sneeze along with his notorious hug of affection.

Felix and Acceptance

Felix accepted his extreme change in lifestyle and seemed to adjust quickly to a world he had never known, wholeheartedly embracing each chance to give and receive. I am sure that if we were able to ask Felix how he would have planned to spend his "golden years," he might have described longer naps and quiet moments in the lap of his beloved Arlene. But life had other plans for this loving little fellow. He would spend his final three and a half years sharing his gifts and loving nature with many new faces everyday—both feline and human—teaching others the value of older pets and bringing joy, laughter, and love to many.

Felix and Appreciation

Felix took and gave the unexpected gifts that followed. This amazing cat's life exemplifies the mysterious and miraculous flow of giving that unfolds and expands when we let go of our specific objective for a particular outcome and instead trust that our gifts will unfold as they should. But Felix's most powerful lesson was still to come. At the age of twenty-three-and-a-half,

Felix developed a severe kidney infection that took his life one morning in July. He was surrounded by all of those who loved him. Although he had lived a full and giving life, we wondered why he could not remain with us for a few more years. The next morning, we received our answer. It came in the form of a phone call from Arlene's daughter. She informed us that her mother had passed away the night before, within hours of Felix's departure. We realized that Felix's giving journey included the role of reuniting with Arlene, his beloved companion of twenty years, just in time to accompany her across Heaven's gate. Felix's story has touched thousands of people throughout the past ten years. Through Felix's journey, we were all given a glimpse into the bigger picture and reminded of the gifts in everything. His life is a perfect lesson. Be who you are, accept others where they are, let life happen, and be open to the gifts. Enjoy the purposeful and joyful life that comes from being guided by your *best self,* and your life may affect others in ways you may never be able to predict.

I am concluding this chapter and this book with my *happy ending story* about those loving senior dogs, Emma and Sammy, who celebrated last year's birthday with me. I previously discussed how these two loving souls awakened my *best self* and brought me immense joy in their presence. In addition to such feelings of love, I also received a glimpse of how powerful the collective hands of *best selves* all working together in love and compassion can be. The day after my birthday, these senior dogs were reunited with their senior owner who was back on her feet again in her new apartment. What a joyous occasion to be part of this reunion! I took pictures of the happy family back together again, and then later that night shared it with everyone who had been part of this special journey to help these dogs and their loving owner. I realized there were fourteen of us who all worked together to keep the dogs safe, healthy, and happy until they would be back where they belonged. There is no doubt in my mind that the love that bubbled over from Sammy and Emma extended to all of us; deeper bonds formed between us as we reveled in the love and happiness that this experience gave us. By combining our unique gifts and efforts, motivated with the common purpose of helping to create a kinder world for all living beings, our happy ending story unfolded and we were moved by their loving natures. Deepening our bonds with each other and strengthening our commitment to help animals, I can see how much the love from Sammy and Emma has already spread to touch more lives. Love unites people and animals, and when people and animals unite, more love is created, and the cycle continues. Simply stated, there is no end to the power of love. It will lead us to the time when we attain that awe-inspiring vision, when our hands will be larger than our hearts' desires and all humans and animals will have the chance to become their *best selves* and live their best lives.

And it all begins within. As you balance your authentic needs with your heart's desires for the animals, and trust your inner wisdom to lead the way, you will be at your best for the animals and for the others with whom you are sharing this privileged journey. Your replenished heart brings longevity and strength to the road that you travel with others who live with a similar passion. And each of us coming together with our unique talents, supporting each other in the sorrow and sharing the joy of success, moves us closer to our shared vision of a kinder world for all living beings. The power of joy in giving to animals is unleashed.

What happens then? Under the guidance of our *collective best selves*, we:

- Work together

- Experience the natural flow of giving to and from the heart

- Support each other as we work toward our shared goals

- Give each other the same extra chances we give to the animals

- Seek to understand our differences and see the gifts in them

- Attract others to join our purpose-driven journey

- Extend our compassion to all living beings

- Become energized, and energize others

- Embrace the gifts of the journey

- Become our *best selves* and grow and expand the collective strength of all of us

- Become a strong, enduring, ever-growing, and unstoppable force that is connected at the core root of our being.

All that we need is already here. Overflowing with joy, take the next step on your love-driven journey. Then, let the power of joy take you, the animals, and all of us to a vision far beyond that which our hearts could ever have imagined.

Works Cited

Gibran, Khalil, (1973) *The Prophet*, New York: Alfred A. Knopf

Kirk, G.S., Raven J.G., & M. Schofield editors, (1984) *The Presocratic Philosophers*, England: Cambridge University Press, Chapter 6

Mitchell, Stephen, (1988) *The Tao Te Ching* by Lao Tzu, New York: HarperCollins

Moore, Thomas, (1992) *Care of the Soul: A Guide to Cultivating Depth and Sacredness in Everyday Life*, New York: HarperCollins

Schweitzer, Albert, edited by Norman Cousins, (1996) *The Works of Albert Schweitzer*, New York: New Market Press, Chapter 4

Shakespeare, William, (2004)(first published in 1600) *The Merchant of Venice*, New York: Simon and Schuster

About the Authors

LINDA R. HARPER, PH.D. has been a clinical psychologist for over thirty years in private practice with her husband in the Chicagoland area. As the founder of *Blessed Bonds*, a foster-based program, and an advocate all of her life, she understands the unique challenges of following one's passion to help the animals. Dr. Harper gives workshops and individual consults on understanding and managing the stress that comes with loving and giving to animals. She is an international speaker and has presented at animal welfare organizations and shelters, veterinarian hospitals, and conferences throughout the country, as well as internationally. She leads the annual *Giving Heart Retreat: Nurturing the Animal Lover's Soul* with Faith Maloney at the Best Friends Animal Sanctuary. She facilitates WINGS, the pet loss support group for the Chicago Veterinary Medical Association.

Dr. Harper is the author of *Eat: A Guide to Discovering your Natural Relationship with Food, Give: A Guide to Discovering the Joy of Everyday Giving, Give to Your Heart's Content . . . Without Giving Yourself Away*, and *The Tao of Eating: Feeding Your Soul through Everyday Experiences with Food.*

For more, visit www.harperhelper.com.

FAITH MALONEY is one of the founders of Best Friends. She is a consultant in all aspects of animal care at the sanctuary, including the Best Friends clinic and adoption programs.

In the early days of Best Friends, Faith spent much of the day in the direct care and feeding of the animals. These days, she devotes an increasing amount of time to helping people from all over the world who are starting sanctuaries themselves. On any given day, at least one group is visiting Best Friends with plans to start a sanctuary or other local animal-care program. Faith co-presents the How to Start and Run an Animal Sanctuary three times a year at Best Friends and co-presents The Giving Heart Retreat with Dr. Linda Harper. Prior to working with Best Friends, Faith was involved with animal care in a small private sanctuary in Pennsylvania, and with counseling and social work in New York and Chicago. She has three children, one of whom is also involved in the work of Best Friends.

Faith was born in England and has a degree in fine art. She also writes articles on animal issues and animal care for Best Friends magazine and other publications.